The Complete
INTAGLIO PRINT

John Ross

Clare Romano

The Complete
INTAGLIO PRINT

THE ART AND TECHNIQUE OF THE INTAGLIO PRINT, THE COLLAGRAPH, PHOTOGRAPHIC INTAGLIO, CARE OF PRINTS, THE DEALER AND THE EDITION, COLLECTING PRINTS, PRINT WORKSHOP, SOURCES AND CHARTS

THE FREE PRESS
A Division of Macmillan Publishing Co., Inc.
NEW YORK

Collier Macmillan Publishers
LONDON

To Christopher and Timothy

THE FREE PRESS
A Division of Macmillan Publishing Co., Inc.

866 Third Avenue, New York, N.Y. 10022

Collier-Macmillan Canada Ltd.

Library of Congress Catalog Card Number: 74-2697

Printed in the United States of America

printing number
1   2   3   4   5   6   7   8   9   10

ACKNOWLEDGMENTS

We are indebted to a number of people whose energies and interest served to help our own. Many artists gave their free time and knowledge in their special areas. They include Peter Milton, Andrew Stasik, Jack Sonenberg, Al Blaustein, Fred and Hilda Castellon, Rudy Pozzatti, Warrington Colescott, Herman Zaage, Michael Ponce de Leon, Herbert Youner and Robert Blackburn.

The basic manuscript was copy edited by Linda Mattison, whose suggestions were thoughtful, constructive and gratefully received. Marie Nolan patiently typed the major portion of the text with assistance from Mary Thompson. We wish to thank Sarah Sprague for compiling the index and checking the photos and captions. Douglas Howell demonstrated the process of making rag paper, Donna Moran of Pratt Institute, Irvil Sloan of Multiples, Donna Stein of the Museum of Modern Art, and Elizabeth Roth of the New York Public Library were all willing with their time and expert help. Valri Pozzatti translated a little known letter from Felicien Rops; Sylvan Cole, Aldis Browne, Estelle Yanco, Hilda Castellon, Candace Brown, Barry Walker, of Associated American Artists Gallery were generous in their assistance; Andrew Fitch and Walter Bareiss, both kind hosts as well as dedicated collectors, were pleasant and informed and shared their enthusiasm with us. Theodore Gusten of I.G.A.S. was cooperative and patient, as were Edna Blank of Andrews/Nelson/Whitehead, and Elke Solomon of the Whitney Museum. Timothy and Christopher Ross were willing models, printers, photo technicians and general assistants. Most of the photographs and all of the drawings are by John Ross, except where noted in the captions. Modernage Photographic Services processed the bulk of the photographs, both in black and white as well as in color. Our special thanks to Lewis Falce, President of Algen Press, for his interest and care in printing the color sections, and to Murray Printing Co. for their fine black and white work.

PRODUCTION CREDITS

This book was designed by Sidney Solomon,
who also planned and supervised the
production through all its stages.
Picture layouts: Bob Vari and Pete Landa
Typesetting: V & M Typographical, Inc.
Printing and binding: Murray Printing Co.
Color printing: Algen Press Corp.

PREFACE

This book is compiled from our larger work, *The Complete Print-maker*, which developed out of our interest in collagraphs in the mid nineteen-sixties. After several assignments as artists-in-residence with the U.S.I.A. exhibition "Graphic Arts U.S.A." in Yugoslavia and Romania, we realized how much interest there was in new methods and approaches in printmaking. There seemed to be little published material on the newer techniques and our students constantly requested information about them. Fellow artists and art historians from various parts of the country wrote to us for details concerning the collagraph, helping to convince us to write down our methods and experiences. Sidney Solomon, whom we first met when he was Director of Design for the Macmillan Company, was involved with the Free Press at that time. He saw our new work and was excited with the new direction and experiments. He prodded us to put some material together for a book on our use of this new technique. He became our editor, designer, and production director, and it was only through his constant interest and encouragement that this book has become a reality.

The emphasis in this presentation is on the workshop approach to printmaking. This postulates that one learns best by doing, and that a flexible approach is more productive than a highly structured, dogmatic sequence of problems designed to impart information in an academic way. The student develops his own ideas at the pace that suits him. An individual artist selects the method that best suits his esthetic intention. It will be helpful to him if he understands the possibilities of other techniques, so that his range of expression can be expanded when necessary. The diversity of work that takes place in a workshop atmosphere is stimulating to many artists, and can create an exciting environment for new and experimental projects. The possibility of combining techniques in a mixed-media statement is enhanced when working in a shop where many methods are being exploited simultaneously. Though small groups are better than very large groups, too few people are also a disadvantage. There should be enough activity in the shop to stimulate ideas and provoke reaction to new directions. In this kind of situation the organization and planning of the workspace is of prime concern; thus we include diagrams and photos.

The present intensity of interest in the fine print is directly related to the advancement of technology in this century. A whole battery of new materials and procedures is open to the adventurous artist who wants to expand his imagery into the world of prints. The print is changing in its technology and, therefore, in its expressive power. The magic of the print becomes that much more intensified with the expansion of means. The artist who is interested in these possibilities must learn to exploit the new procedures and techniques to his advantage.

JOHN ROSS
CLARE ROMANO

CONTENTS

BLACK & WHITE REPRODUCTIONS

COLOR REPRODUCTIONS

FOREWORD

The field of creative printmaking has a rich and varied history of development from its inception to the present time. Yet no period in history can equal the vitality and diversity of growth which has taken place in printmaking in the past twenty years. This growth has been characterized by a myriad of innovative processes and techniques, dynamically new and challenging materials, specially designed hand and power tools, new and better designed presses and most importantly this new interest in the printed image has attracted an ever-increasing number of giftd and dedicated artists throughout the United States.

The full intensity of this growth and development in printmaking has been captured and recorded from the broadest general concept to the minutest significant detail in *The Complete Printmaker*. This excellent definitive volume is the cooperative effort of two highly respected members of the printmaking profession, John Ross and Clare Romano. Both authors have international reputations as creative artists gained from over twenty years of high level production, extensive exhibitions, travel and work abroad and a resultant impressive list of honors and professional recognition. They have played a vital role in the progress and development of printmaking in the United States as artists, teachers and officers in one of this country's most important print organizations, The Society of American Graphic Artists.

I am especially pleased to write this foreword to these special sections of *The Complete Printmaker*, made available in paperback form.

It is most fitting and gratifying that all these meaningful experiences should come together in the form of these volumes dealing with so many aspects of the fine art of printmaking. They are of ultimate value to the professional as well as the novice covering all the major categories of media in explicit detail. There is careful concern for the traditional approach as well as the newest and most inventive. Materials, tools, equipment, processes and techniques are all investigated and defined. The care and collection of fine prints is discussed in fullest detail as is the situation which surrounds the dealer and the establishing and distribution of the edition which so often confounds so many people.

There is a sensitive chapter given to printmaking for children with numerous suggestions, examples and references all of which should facilitate the undertaking and understanding of various aspects of the media on a significant level.

Of invaluable assistance to anyone interested in purchasing tools, materials or equipment or the organization and implementation of a print workshop are the sections devoted to sources, charts and workshops. These sections contain complete, accurate and detailed information on all the necessities for the various media of printmaking and where they may be purchased.

One of the great pleasures of the book is a generous number of exceptionally fine photographs both in black and white and color which are visually exciting and add greatly to the edifying powers of the book.

The premise of these editions is based on the workshop approach—one learns by doing. The workshop environment also promotes a catholic approach to the solution of visual problems in the making of imagery. This book subscribes to the strength of specific or individual media and technique, but it also makes the sense of discovery and the rewards of combining media and techniques clearly apparent.

My friendship and professional involvement with John Ross and Clare Romano is of long standing. This has given me a privileged point of view from which to observe the growth of this book. The work has been long and tedious, but the results are most rewarding.

This is an excellent book which will add immeasurably to the further growth, development and understanding of printmaking. I am honored to give it my own professional approval by this introduction.

Rudy Pozzatti
Distinguished Professor of Art
University of Indiana, Bloomington

Section I

THE INTAGLIO PRINT

INTRODUCTION AND HISTORY

The beginnings of the intaglio process can be traced to the work of 15th-century European craftsmen in metal. Engraving on metal by goldsmiths and armourers was a flourishing art long before the first engravings were printed on paper. Goldsmiths were highly respected, and most of the early engravers who began to experiment with printing on paper had been apprenticed in goldsmiths' workshops. Engraving on paper may very well have evolved out of a need to record a design engraved on a piece of armour or a decorative gold receptacle. According to Hind, the earliest dated print on paper is one from 1446 by an anonymous German engraver known as the Master of 1446, who did a series of *The Passion of Christ*. The first engraver on metal known by name was Martin Schongauer, the gifted German artist whose strong and expressive line and delicate shadings through a network of cross-hatching characterized his work.

In Italy, the art of engraving developed more directly out of the classic ideals of the Renaissance. One of the earliest Italian engravers was a goldsmith named Maso Finiguerra, who worked in silver and gold in a manner called *niello*. In niello work the metal was engraved in line, and the lines were filled with a black substance that gave a strong light-and-dark quality to the metal similar to a printed line engraving. Hind discounts the possibility that the very first prints on paper were made from these niello designs, as scarcely any niello prints go back as far as 1450. He feels it was more likely that niellists began taking impressions of their work on paper after observing the already existing practice among engravers.

Other artists began to engrave in metal specifically for printing. Two methods of working, the *Fine Manner* and the *Broad Manner*, evolved in Florence. The *Fine Manner* used much fine gradation and cross-hatching, and the *Broad Manner* used a freer kind of pen drawing with wide shading. The engraving of Antonio Pollauiolo, *The Battle of the Naked Men*, developed a more personal style. Andrea Mantegna, who produced a great number of engravings, seems to have been an early developer of the atelier system of producing his work, with craftsmen doing most of the engraving. This

Martin Schongauer
"Death of the Virgin" ca. 1471
Engraving 10¼₆" x 6¹¹⁄₁₆"
Metropolitan Museum of Art
Harris Brisbane Dick Fund 1940

1

Albrecht Durer
"The Sea Monster (The Rape of Amymone)" 1498
Engraving 9⅞" x 7½"
Metropolitan Museum of Art
Fletcher Fund, 1919

system was later highly developed by Rubens in Antwerp in the 17th century; he had a large studio of engravers busy reproducing his paintings on plates in order to satisfy a wide popular demand for his engravings.

In Germany, Albrecht Durer used engravings and etching with great inventiveness and richness. His search for classical beauty served as a bridge between the Gothic and the Renaissance. Durer's travels in Italy and his exposure to some of the great Renaissance masters such as Mantegna and Bellini made a lasting impact upon him.

Durer in Germany and Lucas Van Leyden in Antwerp generally worked their plates themselves and produced numerous magnificent engravings of great personal expression. Durer and Van Leyden made some etchings but did not seem to consider it as expressive a means as engraving. Surprisingly enough Durer used the drypoint in three etchings. Hind describes this work as: "the burr of drypoint so completely realized in the St. Jerome that one wonders that Durer did not recur to the method later." Six etchings are also attributed to Durer, though he was not the earliest user of the method. The early etchings were done on iron and lacked the clarity and precision of line found in engravings of the day. There are indications that some engravers used etching as a preparatory means of drawing on the plate to add additional lines to an engraved plate.

Major artists all over Europe were using the new methods of engraving and etching with great skill and creativity. They seemed to exchange information quite readily, though they often suffered when lesser artists copied their plates, as Marcantonio Raimondi in Venice unmercifully copied Durer, down to the famous Durer monogram.

A more expressive use of etching began to be seen in the 16th century. In the landscape etchings of Albrecht Altdorfer, a freer line of varied thickness began to explore the possibilities of space. The use of successive bitings to achieve lines of varying depth soon began to appear in numerous etchings.

However, it was not until the 17th century under the genius of Rembrandt that etchings with flexibility and creative freedom evolved. His work was extraordinary and has not been equaled. More than three hundred plates have come from his hand with a rich variety of subject matter, from landscapes to portraits to biblical compositions.

His innovating plates explored technical and esthetic possibilities unheard of in etching. His use of drypoint in combination with etching produced rich blacks and enhanced his dramatic use of chiaroscuro.

Hercules Seghers, a contemporary of Rembrandt and much admired by him, was a unique artist. His imaginary, panoramic mountain landscapes were far removed from Dutch experience. He was an innovating experimenter and according to Hind was no doubt the first to use color on a copper plate. He seems to have used one color at a time and

Opposite:
Rembrandt van Rijn
"The Descent from the Cross: by Torchlight" 1654
Etching 8¼" x 6⅜"
Metropolitan Museum of Art
Gift of Felix M. Warburg, 1917

Jacques Callot
The Strappado (from The Miseries
and Disasters of War) 1633
Etching 2¾" x 7⅜"
Collection of the authors

achieved additional tints by hand coloring the paper or even the canvas he sometimes used instead of paper. The tinting was done either before or after the impression was made.

After Rembrandt and Seghers, an entire school of portraiture developed in the Netherlands, the etchings of Van Dyck being most noteworthy.

In France the work of Jacques Callot in the 17th century was varied and compelling. His interest ran from direct portraits and military plates to studies of beggars, the *commedia dell'arte* and a unique series, *Miseries of War*. These are a group of small plates showing peaceful villages occupied by tiny figures involved in the horrors of war. This series is probably one of the first statements of protest in the print. Callot's technical achievements were notable in his use of the swelled line in etching and of successive bitings.

After the 18th century there were fewer noteworthy artists working with etching, except for Francisco Goya in Spain, Hogarth in England with engraving and etching, and Tiepolo, Canaletto, and Piranesi in Italy. The visionary work of Goya and his incredible skill with the newly developed aquatint method to enhance his powerful satiric fantasies is carefully studied by students of etching and sought by collectors.

The *Desastres de la Guerra*, Goya's biting reflection on the French occupation of Spain, is one of the great commentaries of all time on the horrors of war and man's inhumanity to man. His *Caprichos* were fanciful, courageous satires of court life and attacked the corrupt court of Charles IV and the Inquisition.

The 19th century, with its obsession with perfection, brought only a steady decline in etching as a creative medium. Great technical proficiency became more and more an end rather than a means.

Later, the artists who developed a new awareness for the beauty of the medium through the artist's own creative exploration of the plate and the printing helped to implement an etching renaissance. One such was Meryon, in France. Towards the end of the century, Whistler, Ensor, and Munch began to use etchings with bold imagination.

The development of the intaglio process in the years since the end of World War II has been almost limitless in inventiveness of image and exploration of technique. The early impetus of Stanley William Hayter's Atelier 17, in Paris before World War II, in New York City during the war, and back in Paris in the post-war years, played a leading role in technical experimentation and the development of unique methods for the use of color. The creative use of the intaglio process in France, England, Germany, Yugoslavia, Poland, and the United States owes much to the heritage of Atelier 17.

INTAGLIO TECHNIQUES

The general term *intaglio* (from the Italian *itagliare*, which means to engrave, carve, or cut) covers a multitude of processes, including engraving, etching, drypoint, aquatint, soft ground, lift ground, mezzotint, and collagraph, as well as a variety of associated techniques. The incised line in the plate holds the ink while the surface is wiped clean. Only the line prints when dampened paper is placed on the plate and both are run through the etching press, with enough pressure to force the paper into the lines.

In an *engraving*, the line is cut into the plate, usually copper or zinc, with a hard steel burin, pushed into the plate by the hand. In *etching*, the line is bitten into the plate with acid wherever the artist has drawn through an acid-proof ground, usually made of wax, lacquer, or asphaltum.

In an *aquatint*, tones are bitten into the plate after the surface has been covered with many tiny droplets of rosin or lacquer. The acid bites the areas around these droplets, producing a tonal effect, which deepens as the plate is left in the acid until the desired tone is achieved.

A *drypoint* line is scratched into the plate with a sharpened needle. In this case the burr of metal thrown up by the point of the tool catches more ink than the line itself. The resulting print makes a rich rough line unlike the crisp hard line of the engraving or etching.

The *soft-ground etching* is made from a plate covered with a ground to which vaseline or tallow has been added. As this ground never really hardens when dry, a variety of textures may be pressed into it, which may be bitten into the plate and then inked and printed.

A *lift-ground etching* requires a clean plate that receives a drawing or painting made with a water soluble ink. A thin coating of liquid wax ground is applied over the entire surface of the drawn plate and the water-soluble ink is soaked off, exposing the plate only where the drawn image has been placed. These lines may be bitten in acid and the plate inked and printed.

A *mezzotint* is made by repeatedly pressing a curved, serrated mezzotint rocker over the surface of a copper plate until it has received many thousands of tiny little indentations from this tool. This procedure is extremely time-consuming, but plates made this way yield rich velvety blacks that can be obtained in no other way. After the entire surface of the plate has been roughened, scrapers and burnishers are employed to achieve tones of grey and white. Mezzotints do not produce large editions because the plates wear out quickly.

A *collagraph* is essentially a print from a collage plate made from a variety of materials which have been firmly glued to a base plate, usually cardboard, hard board, aluminum or other such material. This collage plate is inked by the intaglio method, leaving the recessions or indentations to hold the ink and therefore print when run through the press with dampened paper.

If an uninked plate is run through the press into dampened paper, the resulting impression will be an *embossing*, in which the recessed lines in the plate cause a raised line in the print. If an intaglio plate has the ink rolled onto the surface only, the incised lines will print white, slightly embossed on a solid background. All of these variations are used extensively by contemporary printmakers.

CONCEPT AND IMAGERY

The incised line of the etching plate yields a raised line of ink in the impression that has a crisp, intense, and forceful

Walter Rogalski
"Ladybugs"
Engraving and Mezzotint 24" x 16¾"
Courtesy of the artist

A plate chopper used to cut zinc and copper etching plates at Indiana University.

A small plate cutter at Pratt Graphic Art Center in Manhattan.

Below: A zinc plate is cut to size by Herman Zaage at the New School for Social Research in New York City. The foot treadle operates the cutting blade.

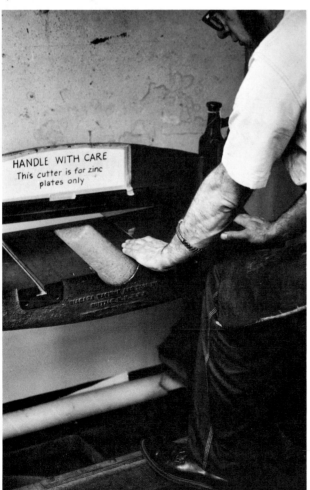

character. This quality has been appreciated by artists who are fine draftsmen and is one of the reasons why some artist-printmakers so love the etching process. The great pressure of the etching press achieves a closer conjunction between the paper and the plate than that of any other graphic process. The plate will show lines of the most sensitive and delicate nature, satisfying the most precise draftsmen over the centuries in which etchings have been made. The medium is also particularly flexible, and changes can be made with relatively minor effort by scraping out those lines that need revision, allowing for repeated redrawing of difficult passages without discarding the rest of the image.

It is possible to ink a single etching plate in many colors to create a color print. It is also possible to print several plates, each inked in different colors, one after the other, in register, on the same impression. There are a number of other ways to create color prints with the intaglio method, but it is easier to achieve color prints by the other graphic techniques, such as screen printing, lithography, and relief printmaking. The time consumed in inking, wiping, and printing an intaglio plate in colors is considerable, and if color is the prime concern you should consider other methods. However, if you want to combine the unique quality of the drawn image and the embossed line with color you may find the intaglio techniques well worth mastering. Many artists use several techniques to achieve color in their prints, such as combining intaglio processes with screen printing or lithography. In most cases the intaglio plates should be printed last to retain the embossment of the lines.

THE PLATE

Zinc and copper are the metals most often used for intaglio plates, with aluminum a distant third because of its brittle quality. As the price of zinc is about one-quarter that of copper, students and beginning printmakers frequently choose the lower-priced metal for their experiments in etching. Brass is occasionally substituted for copper, it bites slowly and very cleanly, and is less expensive than copper. Dutch mordant is used for biting.

Copper is the preferred metal to use for engravings, because of its even texture, uniform ductility, and good printing qualities. It wipes to give a brilliant proof, resists corrosion, and may be steel plated to pull large editions. It is quite expensive, however, and students will find it cheaper to work on photoengraver's zinc. The zinc made today is quite hard, approaching the hardness of copper, because of the alloy structure of the metal. It is more brittle than copper, however, and is not as nice to engrave. It wipes with a slightly muddy effect, and the molecular character of the material makes a brilliant proof more difficult to achieve than with a copper plate. It is a good choice, however, for the beginner. Aluminum and magnesium are poor for engraving because of their brittle texture and should be used only when nothing else is available. Steel has been used for engravings for centuries, and it is still used today in the Bureau of Printing and Engraving in Washington, D.C., to make the engravings for postage stamps. The steel must be soft enough to be cut by the point of the burin. The surface of the plate must be covered with wax or grease when it is stored, or it will rust very quickly. It is not easy to polish a rusted steel plate without weakening fine lines.

When you buy zinc or copper, try to get it directly from the manufacturer or from the supplier who services photo-engraving shops. If you buy it from the art materials supplier you will pay a premium price. The plates come in a variety of sizes, such as 15" by 18", 18" by 20", 20" by 24", 18" by 36", and any variation from these stock sizes involves a cutting and handling charge which can double the per-square-inch price of the basic metal. As the metal is quite easy to cut, a considerable saving can be made by buying the larger sizes and larger quantities of plates. A crate of ten plates can weigh quite a bit, and shipping charges should be ascertained before ordering from a distant supplier.

Cutting Plates

The easiest way to cut a plate, either zinc or copper, is to use a commercial plate chopper, which will be found in every photoengravers shop. Many schools are purchasing this piece of equipment, and if you do a lot of etching on small plates you will appreciate the convenience of the large treadle-operated chopper. A smaller hand-operated model is also in use, but a better buy would be a larger used foot-operated machine, available in larger cities from suppliers to the photoengravers trade. Where floor space is limited, the smaller models may be mounted on a table.

Cutting with a Draw Tool

The most common method of cutting plates is to score them with a draw tool, available from most etching supply houses (see list of suppliers at the end of this book). The draw tool is used as shown. The plate is scored about a dozen times, at first with slight pressure, then with increasing pressure until the groove measures about ⅓ the thickness of the plate. Use a steel T-square or straightedge as a guide and to prevent slipping, at least until the groove is well established, it may be necessary to clamp the straightedge with C clamps on a very large plate. When the groove is deep enough, turn the plate face down along the edge of a table and bend the protruding edge down. If a straight bend appears, the plate will break evenly when it is worked back and forth a couple of times. If the plate simply curves slightly it has not been scored deeply enough, and you must score it further with the draw tool in order to deepen the groove. Most students hate to use this tool because it tends to slip when the groove is first being established.

Cutting with Power Tools

You can cut plates with a carbide-tipped circular saw, but this requires some familiarity with machine tools. We consider this operation dangerous and even more difficult for a beginner to master than a draw tool.

It is possible to score a plate for breaking with a scraper or heavy burin, but this method requires a strong grip and is a last-choice operation to be done only in an emergency.

Cutting a zinc plate with a draw tool requires repeated cuts in the same groove. A steel straightedge is required and it may be clamped in position, if necessary.

After the groove has been deepened sufficiently, the plate will break if it is turned over the edge of a table and bent down and up several times. Do not scratch the surface of the zinc.

The plate should break cleanly along the scored line.

Irregular Shapes

To break a plate into an irregular or indented shape you may use a strong solution of nitric acid to cut through the plate. Paint a solid coat of liquid ground or asphaltum over the plate, scratch the shape on the plate with a blunted needle, allowing about ⅛″ space extra all around, then put the plate into the nitric acid. It will take about two hours in a 3 to 1 or 4 to 1 solution (3 parts water to 1 part nitric acid; see the section on acids) to cut through the plate. You may then bevel the edges with a file or scraper.

Plates may be cut into unusual shapes with a jigsaw or a coping saw. The zinc is soft and cuts easily, while copper needs more time and effort to shape. An acetylene torch will cut through a metal plate in seconds, leaving a molten irregular edge that has a rich textural quality. The propane and butane gas torches used for soldering will not cut fast enough for general use, but they may be helpful when you don't need sharp cutting. Soldered wires and shapes will print well if they are firmly attached to the base plate. Rolf Nesch has used these materials with great distinction.

The easiest way to obtain irregular shapes for intaglio prints is to cut cardboard or paper shapes and to glue them onto the plate with polymer latex gesso. See our description of this technique under "collagraph".

Beveling the Plate

The zinc or copper plate must have its edges beveled to prevent the sharp edge of the plate from cutting through the paper or the blanket. The edge should be angled as shown, which may be accomplished in several ways. You may use files to make the bevel, starting with a coarse file and finishing with a fine file such as a mill bastard. A scraper will work very well. If the scraper makes little ridges or corrugations in the edge, change the angle of cut slightly to reduce them. A patented device used for forming soft metals may also be used. It takes a little longer but produces a very smooth, even bevel. If you start with files and finish with this patented tool, available at Sears, you can make a very smooth edge. Sandpapers and a burnisher, as well as engraver's charcoal, may also be used to smooth the bevel.

The corners of the plate should be rounded to remove sharp points that could catch the wiping tarletan rag or cut your hand if you hand-wipe the plate. All the edges of the plate, including the bottom edges, should be rounded.

Thin plates need no beveling, as the edges are not high enough to cut the paper. Thick cardboard, masonite, and linoleum plates should be beveled to ease the roller over the thick material and prevent the plate from slipping as it is printed. Make sure that the press rollers are adjusted for these extra-thick plates.

LINE ENGRAVING

The technique of engraving with a burin produces a line of crisp, clean edges and a precise character. Areas that require tonality must be built up by a series of closely spaced lines that appear as a tone when enough of them have been

correct bevel — angle to file

Inadequate bevel   BEVELING

The plate should be beveled. One method is to use the scraper to remove the metal. This is a quick and relatively easy chore.

A file may be used to complete the beveling job. In this case a mill bastard is finishing the edge. For rougher work a coarse file is helpful.

engraved. The characteristic swelled line of the engraving, which is thin at the beginning of the stroke and then swells to full strength as the tool bites more deeply, has been highly regarded by artists of earlier years for several reasons. It is capable of yielding a wide variety of effects ranging from delicate to powerful, and engraved plates will produce large editions. As a matter of fact, when etching started to supplant engraving, the early etchers such as Callot used a special tool called the *echoppe* to simulate the engraved line by the process of etching. By rotating this tool in his fingers the artist could start with a thin line and then increase the thickness as the line was drawn.

Line engravings are usually made in copper or zinc, and most engravers prefer copper because of its even texture and ductility. Both metals will yield good prints, although copper wipes to a more brilliant white and, because it is harder than zinc, will produce many more prints. When it is steel-faced it may be printed for hundreds, even thousands, of impressions, a fact dealers have known for many years.

ECHOPPE

Phillippe Mohlitz
"Le Pendu"
Engraving
Fitch-Febvrel Gallery, New York

The burin forces up a sliver of metal or burr. The incised groove is sharp and clean and prints well, for long editions.

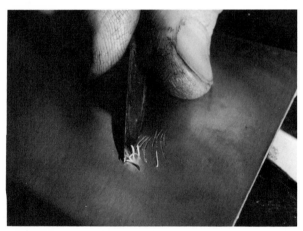

The burr is removed with a very sharp scraper. A dull scraper will scratch the plate. Remove burr as you engrave each line or group of lines. It is very sharp and will cut your hand if not removed.

A multiple tint tool places a series of lines into the plate by the dry point method, i.e., scratching the plate.

Engraving Tools

The basic engraving tool is the burin, a shaft of very hard steel, rectangular in section, which is sharpened at an angle of about 40°. This tool is picked up as shown in the photo. The thumb and the forefinger guide the tool, while the basic forward thrust comes through the palm of the hand. It is important to remember that the plate is pushed into the tool as much as the tool is pushed into the plate. This technique reduces the possibility of slips and gives greater control of the line being engraved. When cutting long sweeping curves, the hand that holds the tool actually moves very little while the other hand pushes the plate into the tool.

Start the line by raising the handle of the burin slightly until the point is driven into the metal. Then lower the handle until it is almost touching the plate. When the plate is pushed into the burin a long sliver of metal will be forced out by the point of the tool. All burrs and raised points of metal should be carefully removed with a very sharp scraper. If these points are not removed, they are hazardous because of their sharpness and will present a problem when the plate is being inked and wiped. They are particularly sharp when the burin is taken out of the line suddenly. If the scraper has not been honed to a very keen edge, it will scratch the plate and cause unpleasant grey streaks where you have used it. These streaks must be removed with engraver's charcoal or a burnisher, which proves that dull tools will always cause trouble. Remember to use the scraper all over the plate. Check thoroughly before printing to avoid painful cuts when hand wiping.

Multiple-cut tools may be used to create tones and textures. These should be sharpened to a very keen edge for metal engraving. The very fine multiples (65 lines or more to the inch) will produce soft greys and blacks.

Frequently an etching will need certain lines strengthened and intensified. Instead of regrounding and re-biting the plate to correct a few lines it will be quicker to use a burin to engrave the lines a little deeper. Remember that an engraved line will print as a very sharp black and may stand out from its etched neighbors with unexpected strength. Be discreet in your use of this technique.

LINE ETCHING

The artist who relies upon fluency of drawing for the realization of his images will find that the etched line offers tremendous advantages over a line drawn with pen and ink. While a pen may occasionally run dry, the etching needle needs no ink to complete its stroke. The needle will not sputter or drip if it is twisted or if its direction is changed suddenly. The thickness of a line may be increased while you are drawing with needles by using a wider point or by leaving the plate in the acid for a longer period of time in order to deepen and widen the line.

Tones and textures are easy to get with aquatint and soft-ground techniques, and these can be used to enhance the line work or to add shapes and tonal areas to the image. An etched line can vary from the faintest scratch to a deep black stroke ⅛" wide. Even wider lines may be obtained by using multiple strokes or by the lift-ground process.

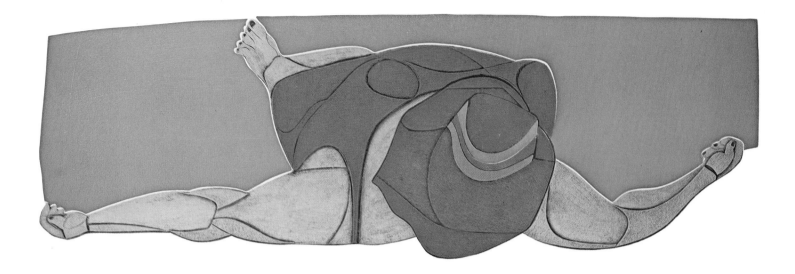

Clare Romano
"On the Grass"
Color collagraph 10¼" x 30¾"
Collection Museum of Modern Art, New York
One cardboard plate cut into six segments, inked separately with 9 colors in intaglio and relief, reassembled on the press and printed in one run through the press.

John Ross
"Quadros XII" 1969
Color collagraph 20" x 20"
Collection New Jersey State Museum
Two plates are used for this print, each one inked in five or six colors. The second plate is printed in register on top of the first impression while the ink and paper are still wet.

Warrington Colescott
"Snapshots from Underground" 1971
Color intaglio and screenprint 41½" x 29½"
Associated American Artists Gallery

Gabor Peterdi
"Lanikai Sundown" 1971
Combined techniques, segmented plate intaglio, relief,
drypoint, soft ground 34½" x 21¾"
Courtesy of the artist

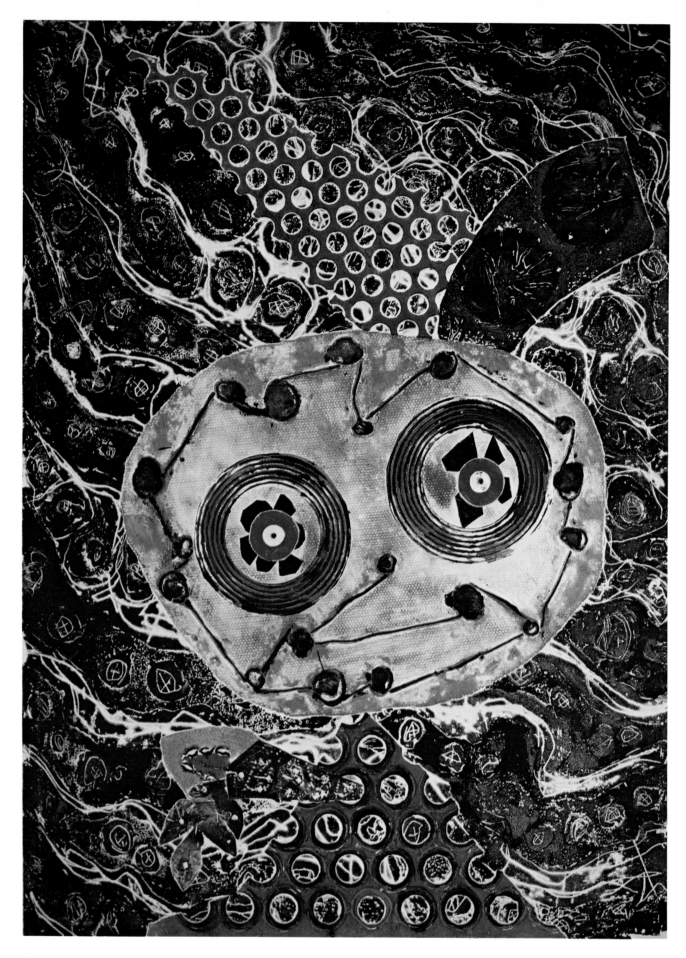

Rolf Nesch
"Toy" 1965
Metal collage print 22⁹⁄₁₆" x 16½"
Collection Walter Bareiss

Jacek Gaj
"Dance" 1965
Etching
Pratt Graphics Center

It is easy to draw through a wax ground with a needle, so easy, in fact, that this process is normally learned first when you are approaching the intaglio technique. It is more difficult to control a drypoint line and far more difficult to achieve success with line engraving. A variety of tools have been used to draw through the ground. Almost anything that will remove the ground will suffice as an etching needle. To make a dark area with lines alone will require many lines close together, usually cross-hatched and often bitten in the acid in several applications of cross-hatching. Rembrandt has used this process with power and sensitivity, and his prints may be studied with great reward to the beginning etcher. If lines that are closely spaced are left too long in the acid, they will fuse together and eventually lose their individual character. Dense blacks are achieved only through multiple biting of many cross-hatchings, with each series of lines bitten properly.

Materials

Zinc or copper photoengraver's plates
Needles (old dental tools are good)
Hard ground and roller *or*
Liquid ground and 1" or 2" flat brush
Nitric acid and glass storage bottles
Plastic tray for acid (large enough for plate)
A glass measuring cup for preparing acid solutions
Mineral spirits (such as benzine or varnoline for diluting and cleaning the ground)
A watch or a clock for timing the bite
A triangular scraper (for removing errors)
A curved burnisher (for burnishing and polishing errors and lightening aquatints)

Liquid ground should be flowed onto the plate with a wide soft brush. The ground should drain to a thin even coat, when it can be placed on the hot plate for a minute to speed drying. Do not overheat the ground, or it will false bite.

ETCHING GROUNDS

Liquid Grounds

The acid-resistant covering that protects the plate is called ground. There are many formulas for making grounds, and many different types are available for purchase. Only those grounds that use chemicals available today will be discussed. The exotic chemicals of past ages are difficult to obtain; there is little advantage in knowing a formula that specifies the use of "Rosin of Tyre" if you can't find it.

The most commonly used ground is a liquid ground, painted on the plate with a wide, flat, soft brush. Although several companies manufacture this type, it is easy to make a large batch and bottle it for future use. The ingredients are easily obtainable.

2 parts asphaltum
2 parts beeswax
1 part rosin (powdered)

All ingredients are dissolved in varnoline or benzine of low volatility. Although heating hastens the process, the penetrating odor requires excellent ventilation; and the danger presented by a pot full of hot ground, which is quite inflammable, makes it prudent to recommend the slower but safer method, without heat. Asphaltum is usually obtained in a liquid state and is usually added last to the mixture of rosin and wax. As the rosin is hardest and slowest to dissolve, it is placed in benzine or varnoline first and allowed to dissolve, with occasional stirring. The beeswax is added next, along with more varnoline. The usual procedure is to make the ground somewhat thicker than required and then to add solvent to each batch as you use it. Good ground will take an amazing amount of solvent without being over-thinned. A little heat will speed the drying process after the ground is on the plate.

Several commercial grounds made with ether or chloroform as a solvent are available. These dry very quickly and are not brushed on but poured over the tilted plate. The plate is then twirled or spun quickly in order to spread the ground rapidly over the entire surface. It takes only a few seconds to cover the plate. When these grounds are dry they are very slick and hard and may be handled quite a bit without damage. Such a ground may be used as a stop-out varnish because it dries so quickly. As it tends to feather or bleed, however, you must be careful with it. The cost of commercial grounds is very high, and most artists will find that making their own ground will be much cheaper.

Asphaltum, thinned with varnolene or mineral spirits may be used as the ground if the work to be done doesn't have fine lines. Asphaltum will flake off if it is too thin and is no substitute for a good liquid ground. However it is an excellent ground for very long deep biting and when cutting through a plate.

To apply a hard ball ground, the plate should be heated on the hot plate until the ground melts and may be spread evenly with a hard roller. This roller is made of hard linoleum. Hard rubber may be used if the plate is not too hot. Soft rubber and gelatine are not suitable for this work.

Hard Ground

Hard ground is more difficult to make than liquid ground because it must be heated to melt the ingredients together. The ingredients are the same as for the liquid ground but omit the solvent. As several companies sell good hard ground (called ball ground because it looks like a dark ball about the size of a golf ball) you can buy it quite easily. Webers, Cronite, and Graphic Chemical all have hard ground at reasonable prices.

The etching plate must be heated on an electric or gas hotplate to melt the ground sufficiently to spread it easily. Do not overheat it, or the wax will bubble, smoke, and burn. The ground may be rolled over the warm plate to a smooth, even, transparent coat. A roller of hard rubber may be used if the plate is not allowed to become too hot. A linoleum roller is very handy, but hard to find. Leather rollers are still available from Craftool or Rembrandt Graphic Arts Co., although expensive. Soft rubber or gelatine rollers should not be used to spread hard grounds because they will melt or be deformed by the heat.

I have seen dabbers used so skillfully to apply a ball ground that the wax appeared to be absolutely even over the entire plate. The plate should be warmed just enough to melt the ground, then rapidly worked over with short, dabbing strokes. The heat will distribute the wax over the surface. A dabber may be made easily from a piece of umbrella cloth or fine silk, some cotton, and a 3″-diameter disk cut from two or three pieces of cardboard.

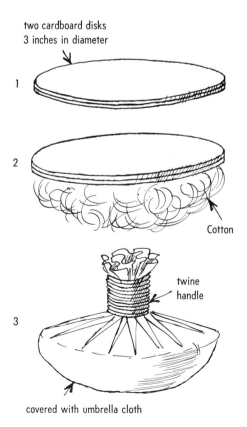

two cardboard disks
3 inches in diameter

1

2

Cotton

3

twine
handle

covered with umbrella cloth

MAKING A
DABBER

A plate is smoked using an overhead rack made from wire coat hangers to support the zinc. The rack is hung from the ceiling on wires.

A card is used to draw into a soft-ground. The edge will pick off the ground where it touches the plate, and these lines may be bitten in the acid.

Below: To obtain a line drawing in soft-ground, place a piece of textured paper under your drawing next to the soft-grounded surface.

Very Hard Liquid Ground

A very hard, thin, transparent, durable liquid ground may be made by diluting Heims Steel Etching Ground with an equal quantity of lacquer thinner. This ground, which ordinarily dries too quickly to brush out evenly, will dry a little more slowly when mixed with the lacquer thinner. Mix only enough for each separate use. To find where the basic ground is available, see the list of suppliers at the end of the book.

All liquid grounds should be applied with a wide soft brush to a tilted plate, which lets the ground flow across the plate and drain to a thin even coat. Placing the plate on a heater, for a few seconds only, will hasten the drying process.

Staging Ink Ground

A hard, tough ground may be made by using staging ink, a commercially prepared compound sold by photoengravers' supply houses, such as H. Pitman. It is brushed evenly over the plate, then heated to about 250° or 300° F., over an electric hotplate. It may be removed with mineral spirits.

Smoking the Ground

Occasionally it is helpful to transfer your drawing onto a blackened plate, in order to see the drawing better and to see the lines as you open them with the needle. The color of most grounds is close to that of copper, and it is not easy to see what you have drawn when you use copper.

The traditional method of blackening a plate is to smoke it with the carbon deposit of a candle or taper. The plate must be warmed to soften the ground so that the carbon will color it completely and not simply remain on the surface. Use a small hand vise to grip the edge of the plate, cushioning the jaws of the vise with a few pieces of cardboard to prevent scratches. Warm the plate over a hotplate or a gas burner, but don't cause the ground to bubble or smoke. Light a taper or candle that will smoke and pass the candle under the plate, grounded side to the flame. You may use a wick and a glass jar containing kerosene, grease, or vaseline. Move the flame constantly, and don't touch the ground with the wick. The carbon deposited on the ground should fuse with it and form a solid black coat that will not rub off. Your needle will now make lines that are plainly visible. An overhead support made of wire coat hangers will enable you to smoke large plates with ease.

Stop-Out Varnish

Any acid-resisting compound that dries quickly may be used as a coating to prevent certain areas from further etching in the acid solution. Quick-drying ether or chloroform-based grounds may be used. Hard ground is always handy, and when length of drying time is not too important a factor, it makes a suitable stop-out. Asphaltum is frequently used, as it is kept in every etcher's shop. Commercial stop-out varnish is usually alcohol-based, with rosin and coloring dissolved in it.

When it is necessary to bite the plate very deeply, you may protect unbitten areas of the plate by covering them with Contact paper. This is a plastic sheet with an adhesive backing. The plastic resists the acid.

Soft Ground

A soft ground, even when dry, remains soft and sensitive to pressure. Different textures may be impressed into it, and these textures may be bitten by the acid into the plate. You make soft ground by adding vaseline to liquid hard ground and mixing thoroughly. About one part vaseline to three parts ground by volume is correct, depending upon the softness desired. Other materials, such as tallow or lard, may be mixed with hard ground. In such recipes you should add more of the soft material to the liquid ground, up to equal volumes of each. Vaseline is more easily obtainable at any drug store, and its composition is more dependable than either tallow or lard.

Soft ground should be applied by a wide smooth brush to a very thin even film. The sensitivity of the ground changes as it thickens, and an irregular ground will give uncertain textures.

A paste soft ground made by Weber's is available in supply stores in the New York area and is very easy to apply. Heat the plate moderately, dab a few spots of paste onto the plate, and roll it out to a thin even film with a moderately soft roller. Do not use a plastic or gelatin roller on the warm plate, because the heat will injure the roller.

Soft-Ground Techniques

The classic method of working in soft ground is to draw through a thin sheet of textured paper, such as pastel paper or thin watercolor paper, onto a plate that has been covered with soft ground. As this ground remains sensitive to the touch even after it is dry, the plate must be handled with care. A fingerprint will be bitten, and other slight scratches and bruises will show. Make a bridge from a piece of thin plywood, as shown, to keep your hand away from the surface as you draw. The textured surface of the paper will pick up the soft ground from the plate. If you use a hard pencil or ballpoint pen, the line will be relatively thin, but if you use a blunt stick or the curved end of a burnisher the line will be fairly wide. The line will have the characteristic pebbly texture of the paper after the plate has been bitten in the acid. You may tape your sketch, which can be on thin tracing paper, to the table in position over the grounded plate. Then various papers of different textures can be slipped between the sketch and the plate to get a variety of textures in the lines.

You can use fabrics and materials of different weaves and textures by placing them on the plate in the desired position on the soft ground. Run the plate through the press, with pressure somewhat less than used for printing. Put a piece of waxed paper or newsprint on top of the fabric to protect your blankets from the soft ground, which may be forced through the porous fabric. You can use corduroy, burlap, denim, lace, linen, and other fabrics, as well as pieces of paper, cardboard, gasket material, cork, string, or

When using soft-ground it is wise to employ a "bridge" to raise your hand away from the sensitive surface. Draw with heavy pressure to make sure that the paper will press down into the ground and remove it from the plate.

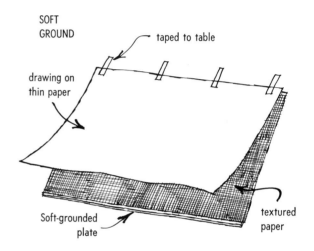

SOFT GROUND — taped to table — drawing on thin paper — Soft-grounded plate — textured paper

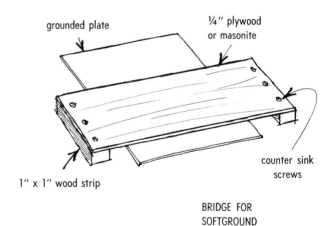

grounded plate — ¼" plywood or masonite — counter sink screws — 1" x 1" wood strip

BRIDGE FOR SOFTGROUND

Below: You may use pencils, sticks, or any other kind of stylus as a drawing instrument.

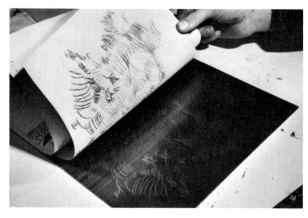

When you check your plate be sure that the textured paper has been forced through the soft-ground, exposing the metal. Varying the pressure will give different weights to the lines. Increasing the length of the bite in the acid will also darken the lines.

Textured fabrics may be pressed into a soft-grounded plate with a hard rubber roller.

Grasses and plants may be impressed into a soft-ground. Here they have been run through the etching press, with the pressure somewhat reduced from printing pressure. Protect your blankets with waxed paper or smooth newsprint.

Below: When the grass and plants have been removed, their impression has been forced into the soft-ground. The plate should be bitten in acid without delay because the surface is receptive to all sorts of pressure and accidental smudges easily occur.

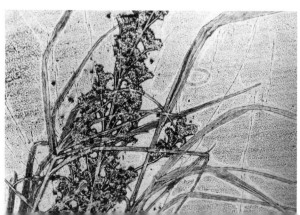

any other found items. You may touch the ground with any object to make an impression of that object's shape in the soft ground. If you don't want certain areas to bite, stop them out with ground, asphaltum, or varnish before you immerse the plate in the acid. It is possible to use the point of a needle in the same way as you would when working on a hard ground. The line will be sharp and clean after biting. In fact, the soft ground is very useful when you are reworking a plate that has already been bitten. The soft ground clings to the irregularities of the etched plate better than the normal hard ground and prevents foul biting around the edges of deeply bitten lines.

AQUATINT

The process of aquatint should be mastered by every printmaker who intends to do serious work in etching. The wide variety of greys, ranging from delicate, light washes to rich, deep blacks are indispensible to an artist who needs tonality in his work. The principle of aquatint is simple. A fine mist of acid-resistant tiny droplets or particles of acid-resistant material is dusted or sprayed over the zinc or copper plate. When this mist is fixed to the surface it should cover about 40% of the area. Place the plate in a weak solution of nitric acid. The usual proportions range from 1 part of nitric acid in 8 parts of water to 1 part acid in 12 parts of water. The design is put on the plate by protecting those parts that are to appear white with an acid-resisting ground or stop-out. The acid will attack the unprotected portions of the plate and not the tiny spots that are covered by the droplets. The darkness of the tone is increased by leaving the plate in the acid solution for longer periods.

Below: The typical white dots where the acid has been resisted shows clearly in this enlargement of a print by John Ross. A coarse spray paint was used. The black lines are through a soft ground, the white lines are acrylic polymer gesso.

The Rosin Dust Method—Hand Applied

Finely ground rosin may be dusted over the plate from a small cloth bag that is shaken or tapped from a short distance above the plate. This dusting should be done in a draft-free place and practiced until a fairly even dusting of rosin can be applied to the plate. The bags can be made from several layers of fine nylon stockings or fine broadcloth. You should be able to control the quantities of rosin powder by flicking the bag with your fingers.

The fineness of the powder will affect the texture of the aquatint tone. If the powder is coarse, the larger particles of rosin will cause larger white dots to appear in the finished print. When a coarse tone is needed you may have to crush lump rosin with a mortar and pestle to the right consistency. The prepared powdered rosin is always ground to very fine powder. It will be helpful to have several bags of rosin of varying degrees of coarseness at hand for a wide latitude of textures in the tones.

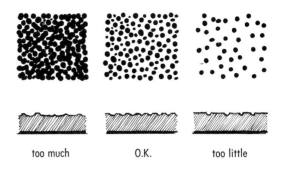

too much   O.K.   too little

AQUATINT COVERAGE

Francisco Goya
"Disparate Furioso" (No. 6 Los Proverbios)
Etching and Aquatint 8½" x 12¼"
Collection Jacob Landau

To make an aquatint bag, place few spoonfuls of rosin powder on a square of porous cloth.

Fold up the corners of the cloth square and tie with string or a rubber band. Different degrees of coarseness can be kept in separate bags. The coarser grind will require a coarser mesh fabric.

Flick the aquatint bag with your finger to force the powder through the mesh of the cloth. Experiment in a place free of drafts or sudden breezes. An even misting of rosin powder is essential.

Top, right: An aquatint box, operated by compressed air to blow rosin particles into the air. The shelf on which plates are placed is visible through the glazed front. Indiana University.

Bottom, right: Aquatint chamber at Cooper Union, New York City. An electric fan blows the rosin particles into the air.

Rosin Dust Method—Dust Boxes

The best control over an aquatint tone is obtained by a dust box, which can be constructed in several ways, each of which requires a ledge or open shelf near the bottom of the box upon which to place the plate. The principle of the box is to contain a cloud of rosin dust, which will settle evenly over the plate. This cloud of rosin can be raised with a hand bellows or a motor-driven fan. The plate is not placed on the shelf immediately, but only after the heavier particles of rosin are allowed to settle. The finer particles will float longer in the air in the box and drop more slowly to the bottom. This process allows great control over the evenness of the tone.

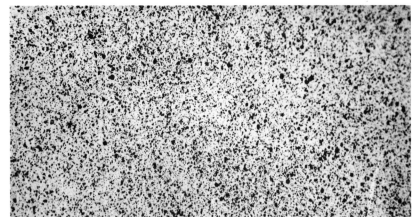

The rosin particles darken to an amber color when they are hot enough to fuse to the plate. The plate should be heated just enough to cause the rosin to adhere to it. Too much heat will melt the rosin into an impervious coat that the acid cannot evenly penetrate. *Above, right:* The proper amount of particles for an aquatint should cover about 40% of the surface of the plate. This coverage is from a can of pressure-spray enamel.

Below: A zinc plate, bitten in fresh 8-1 nitric acid, yields tones as shown in this test proof. Paint spray was used for the aquatint.

Another method for agitating the rosin powder is to revolve the entire box on a pivot, placing the plate on its shelf when the larger pieces of rosin have settled. The disadvantage of this method is that the large plates in use today make the revolvable box a very cumbersome affair. A simpler solution would seem to be found in the bellows or fan-operated box.

In each case a window made of plastic, plexiglas, or glass is necessary to enable you to view the plate to check the quantity of dust that has settled on it. The plate must be removed when it is properly covered.

All rosin-dust aquatints must be adhered to the plate by heating. A hotplate that can reach a temperature hot enough to melt rosin, 300° to 400° F., must be used. Electric heat is safer than a gas flame, but either type will work. The rosin will turn to an amber color when it is hot enough to stick to the plate. By constantly turning the plate you can keep the rosin from burning or melting into a solid layer. It must be evenly heated. Viewing the plate from the edge will enable you to judge the color of the rosin more exactly. You should wear heavy gloves when handling heated plates. If the aquatint powder has not adhered firmly to the plate, it will float off when placed in the nitric acid, and the tone will be spoiled.

The Paint Spray Aquatint

A very rapid method of obtaining an aquatint is to spray the plate with a fine mist of enamel paint from a pressurized paint can. With a little practice this procedure can be made practically foolproof. It is particularly useful when light and middle-value grey tones are needed. Start spraying off to the side of the plate to be sure the spray is working well, then spray the plate, and stop spraying only after the plate has been passed. Work back and forth in a regular pattern, holding the can about 12″ to 14″ away from the plate surface. Experiment with various brands of paint until you find one that sprays a mist fine enough to suit you. Some brands will spray little drops, which will cause coarse white speckles in your printed tone. Do not use spray cans when they are nearly empty, as they tend to sputter and spatter irregular drops.

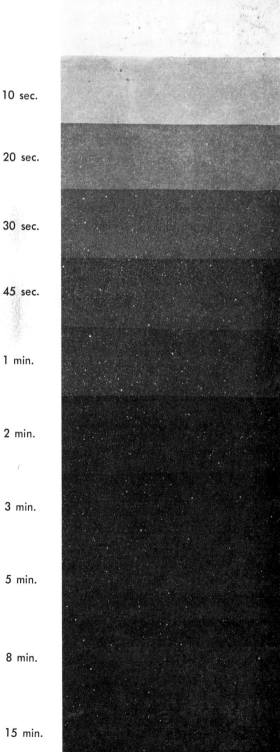

10 sec.

20 sec.

30 sec.

45 sec.

1 min.

2 min.

3 min.

5 min.

8 min.

15 min.

The advantage of spray paint is that it dries almost instantly and does not have to be heated. The disadvantages are that the spray is smelly and the fumes may be dangerous. A very long bite in the acid may wash off the particles of paint, so that the deeper black tones may require a heated rosin aquatint. Only your own experiments will determine what best suits your requirements.

Stopping Out Aquatints

You may use hard ground or stop-out varnish to stop out those parts of an aquatinted plate that are not to be bitten. The plate is normally covered completely with the dust or spray before the design is painted on top, although it is possible to paint the design first and apply the dust or spray later. The possibility of ruining a complicated drawing with a poorly applied aquatint is always present and heat needed in a rosin aquatint may melt the ground. Therefore, it is prudent to do the aquatinting first. All parts that are to appear white must be covered with ground or varnish before the biting. A light grey tone can be bitten into a zinc plate in 10 seconds if it is placed in 8:1 nitric acid solution. The longer you leave the plate in the acid, the darker the tone gets. After 3 minutes in the acid the tone is quite dark (about 85% of black), and it gets darker very slowly, taking 10 or more minutes to develop into a rich, dark value. If you have covered too much of the plate with particles of rosin or paint, it may never develop a really deep tone.

Quick-drying grounds, such as ether or alcohol-based grounds, are not suitable for delicate linear stop-outs because they tend to feather or spread when applied to the aquatint plate. Any acid-resisting varnish will work, if you understand how to use it. In general, weak acids and slow biting are better because they allow for careful control, but the artist may want to use strong acid for a rough accidental effect and then develop the image from there.

In general zinc plates are so much softer than copper that they yield far fewer prints, particularly in the case of aquatints. You will find that zinc aquatints will start to weaken and the prints become lighter and lighter after only 20 to 50 impressions. If you need long editions, use copper plates, bitten in ferric chloride or Dutch mordant, and steel-face them. With this process, a very thin coating of chromium is electrolytically deposited over the entire surface of the copper plate. This coating is very hard and resists wear better than the copper. It may be renewed several times to prolong the life of valuable plates.

Sandpaper Aquatints

A grey tone may be obtained by using sandpaper instead of rosin or paint, although the quality of the tone may not be as fine or even. The procedure is simple. Place a thin coat of hard ground over a plate and let it dry. Put the plate face up on the bed of your etching press, cover the plate with a piece of medium sandpaper, and run it through the press with the pressure reduced. It may be necessary to run the plate and sandpaper through several times in different positions to assure an even tone. The particles of sand puncture the ground, allowing the acid to bite the plate in those

When an aquatint is bitten correctly the texture is even. The outside of these shapes was impressed into soft-ground and bitten very deeply. The center left area is aquatint; the right side is soft-ground texture.

points. Technically the effect is the reverse of the rosin aqua-tint, but the tones look similar to the eye. The stopping-out procedures are the same as before. A drypoint quality can be achieved by placing the sandpaper over a clean plate without ground and running it through the press.

White Effects and Soft Edges on Aquatints

You may use a grease or wax crayon to draw directly on the aquatinted plate before it is bitten, in order to get a soft white line. Press hard enough to deposit the wax or grease on the plate, where it acts as a resist to the acid. Melted rosin, which is quite hard and durable, is better than spray paint, which is delicate and easily damaged. The best crayons are soft litho crayons, children's wax crayons, cray-pas, or even wax candles. You can soften hard edges this way, too. If you want aquatint to fade gradually into a white background, fine sandpaper may be used to soften the edge.

Flour of Sulphur Method

For delicate wash effects, the flour of sulphur method is very easy and produces soft, pale tones. You need only olive oil and precipitated sulphur powder, called flour of sulphur, which you may keep in an old saltshaker. Use the olive oil as a paint, placing it directly on the surface of the plate where you want the tone. Shake the sulphur powder into the oil, blow off the powder where it has fallen on undesired places, and then let the plate sit for a few hours. The sulphur will bite into the plate, but to a very shallow depth, which may wear rapidly but produces delicate soft tones of grey.

LIFT-GROUND PROCESS

This process enables you to use the intaglio plate for the liveliest, most autographic brushed line or mass that you can produce. It is a direct process; if you paint a black line on a plate, you get a black line on the print. The design is brushed on with a water-soluble paint. There are several formulas that work well. Picasso used a solution of sugar melted in boiling water, colored it with a tube of black gouache or watercolor, and finally added gamboge, a photoengraver's compound, that dissolves readily in water. Other usable formulas are as follows:

> 10 parts Karo syrup
> 2 parts black India ink
> 1 part powdered soap
> 1 part powdered gum arabic

Another formula for lift ground is:

> 10 parts simple syrup (1 part
> sugar to 5 parts water
> boiled to a syrup)
> 3 parts black poster color
> 2 parts detergent
> (gum arabic is optional)

The use of poster paint alone is inadvisable because the bind-ers in the paint do not dissolve as completely as you would

A lift ground is washed out in water, with a soft brush hastening the process.

A solution of water and gum arabic or non-crawl is painted on to a zinc plate that has an aquatint ground on its surface.

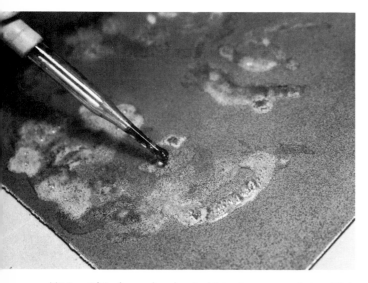

Nitric acid is dropped or brushed into the water painting. Nitric acid in varying solutions may be brushed directly on the plate. The drops should be dispersed instantly or they will bite in a spotty manner.

wish. It must be mixed with gamboge, soap, or gum arabic to help it dissolve. Do not attempt to use the paint too thinly or in wash effects. It should be quite thick as it flows from your brush. You can also use a pen or dip fabric or other textured material into the solution and then place it on your plate.

It is imperative that the plate be absolutely free of grease, or the paint will not stick. Clean the plate thoroughly with detergent and wipe dry. If this doesn't work, immerse the plate completely in a dilute solution (8:1 or weaker) of nitric acid for a second or two, then wash it in running water and wipe dry. The surface may be mottled, but it will be grease-free. Acetic acid will work, but it requires a few more seconds than nitric. When the plate is clean you may complete your design, painting the positive areas you want to print. When your drawing is dry, apply a thin liquid hard ground over the entire plate. It must be thin and even, not at all lumpy or uneven. When it has dried, put the plate into a tray of water and let it soak for a while. You will see that the lift solution will dissolve slowly, leaving the plate exposed wherever you have painted your design. You can gently brush the surface of the plate to hasten the process. Do not be in too much of a hurry, but let it soak a little longer rather than take the chance of scratching the plate. Eventually the complete drawing will be exposed.

If the plate is bitten in acid now, the lines will be lowered as the levels of zinc or copper are removed, but it is really necessary to aquatint the plate in order to achieve the darks that you may desire. It is advisable to employ the spray paint aquatint technique rather than the heated rosin aquatint method. Make sure that the spray can is adequately filled and that the nozzle is not clogged. Try it on the back of the plate before spraying the grounded surface. This is no time to overspray, thereby flooding the drawing with paint and ruining it. The spray should be evenly applied with about 40% coverage of the surface. It is easier to apply a spray aquatint than to heat a rosin-dust aquatint with the possible damage to the ground. Check it under an engraver's glass. Bite the plate as for a normal aquatint. You may vary the darkness of the greys by stopping out and biting for various lengths of time.

Spit-Bite Aquatint

The hard edge of the lift-ground aquatint can be varied in a number of ways. A dry brush effect, achievable with a partially charged brush, can cause a grainy texture that will soften the stroke of the brush. Another way to cause variations in the tone is to use a procedure commonly called spit-bite. Delicate wash effects with soft, graded edges are possible with this method. The process does not require a lift-ground procedure, although the best control over the drawing is obtained that way.

There are several ways of working with spit-bite. The strongest effects require that the plate be given an even tone of aquatint spray or powdered rosin, fused well to the surface. It is possible to work directly on this surface by painting with water to which a little noncrawl (Dr. Martin's Flex-Opaque) has been added. You can tint the water with dye or watercolor to make it easy to see. After you have painted a small area with water, drop some pure nitric acid into the water deposited by your brush strokes. Be careful not to let large drops give your line a spotty effect. It is possible to flow the acid on smoothly with a small eye-dropper, an old brush, or even cotton swabs or Q-tips. The acid will bite quickly, and in a minute or less it will have bitten the strokes into the plate.

It is possible to paint directly onto the plate with pure acid, but the action of the mordant is so strong that it may undercut the rosin or paint drops. This deep groove will cause the area to bite as a crevé (without texture), and it will therefore not print as dark. It seems strange that dilute acid will bite a darker grey than pure acid, but that is the case. It is difficult to control the tonalities with this process, however, and several bitings may be necessary.

The best control with this biting technique is obtained when you put the drawing on the plate with a lift-ground procedure, then spray or fuse an aquatint mist over the plate, and then paint with water on the exposed areas. Paint the pure acid into the water with a brush. Your tones will resemble a wash drawing with irregular variations of texture and tonalities. Burnishing to lighten certain strokes is very effective because the aquatint is not deeply bitten and responds quickly to the burnisher. Sanding with fine sandpaper and then working with the burnisher will quickly lighten the tone of lift-ground acquatints to obtain wash effects and soft edges and, in conjunction with the spit-bite, can produce delicate wash tints.

Felicien Rops, in a long letter to the printer-artist Delatre, describes his methods for making aquatints and soft grounds by using a variety of textured papers to avoid a monotonous uniformity in the soft-grounded plate. Rops also uses a form of spit-bite on these plates, applying the acid with a large brush to those areas that he wishes to etch into the plate. He draws test lines in the margins of the plate, having taken care to make his plate a little larger than necessary. These test sketches are etched, then the ground removed just from those spots, in order to check the depth of the bite. When the sketches seem satisfactory, Rops proceeds to draw in the classic soft-ground manner on the remainder of the plate. Rops preferred to etch these subtle plates in bichromate of potassium or in Dutch mordant.

Peter Milton's Procedure

Peter Milton has used the lift-ground method with extraordinary skill and patience. He has described his procedure so thoroughly that we are presenting this letter he wrote describing his work on "October Piece."

"I draw the image directly on an ungrounded, scrupulously clean copper plate (zinc can be used) with pen and sugar-ink. Some of the more textural areas I put on with tissue paper and then refine them extensively. In *October Piece* the grass areas were started with a paint roller and sugar-ink. One of the greatest advantages of sugar-ink is that it can be easily removed during the shaping of the images and the modification of texture. It can be either flaked off or removed with a damp tissue. But all traces of

This plate was bitten with spit bite only. Five separate sprays of aquatint were used.

Felicien Rops
"Maturite"
Soft ground etching 9" x 6¹³⁄₁₆"
Collection of the authors

Peter Milton
"October Piece" 1970
Lift ground etching 17¾" x 23⅞"
Courtesy of the artist
Photo Eric Pollitzer

sugar must be removed in the latter case or the whole area will later lift.

"I make the sugar-ink by dissolving enough sugar in heated India ink to make a heavyish syrup when it cools, and I then dilute it to workable consistency by adding more ink. In low humidity conditions a few drops of glycol antifreeze retards drying and improves the handling of the ink. I use a Hunt #107 hawk quill and #104 mapping points, with the point often touched up and refined with polishing paper as a sharpener. The point must be cleaned often to keep the ink flowing freely.

"When the drawing is finished the plate is covered with an extremely dilute (benzine) hard-ground using Peterdi's formula. The ground must be even, and I have found a bubble level useful in leveling the plate to even the settling of the liquid. I use a 2″ white bristle brush. If there is any streaking of the liquid it will be due to the ground's not being dilute enough. It should be very gratifying to know that one has many chances to get the ground perfect. If after drying the ground seems too thick (will not lift well), too thin (will false bite), too uneven, or too rough with impurities, the plate can be flooded with benzine and cleaned with a very soft absorbent material without injuring the drawing. I usually try 5-8 times before I am satisfied.

"The plate is then placed in a tray of hot water, just hot enough to be uncomfortable to the hand, and left until the water has cooled to room temperature. The sugar in the ink reacts with the water and swells, so that the ink softens; the ground over it loosens and may be rubbed away by hand. The plate is methodically and vigorously rubbed until the metal is. exposed at every point that there was a sugar-ink mark. There is no mark so delicate that it shouldn't lift if everything has gone right.

"I etch the plate in the manner normal for copper, with Dutch mordant and many stopping-out steps, using rosin/alcohol/methyl violet dye as the stop-out varnish. Any mark or shape too broad to hold ink well during the printing can be strengthened. Since a heated aquatint is likely to foul the ground, I either spray on a rosin/alcohol solution through an atomizer or use a commercial paint spray, such as Krylon flat-black enamel.

"Later I add much straight engraving with the burin to refine the image, and it is at this stage that the figures take on their rather photographic quality. I do not use photo-engraving aids and, while this is impractical, it is curiously satisfying. I do use photographs extensively, but only to draw from. In October Piece I spent around 3-4 months on the pre-acid drawing stage and 2-3 months on the post-acid engraving.

"It must be said that this approach as I am using it is probably as antithetical as can be conceived to the more-or-less contemporary printmaking concepts which emphasize openness to materials and to the medium itself. As much as anyone, I would hate to see such procedures as I have just outlined lead us back to the kind of frozen tedium that afflicted printmaking for so many years before its present health."

Mario Avati
"Des Oeufs pour ta Fete" 1960
Mezzotint 8⅝" x 10⅞"
Collection Manhattanville College

MEZZOTINT

Few contemporary artists have the time to rock a plate with a mezzotint rocker long enough to produce the velvety black impression so characteristic of the best work. Mezzotint is a drypoint method, with the rocker digging into the surface of the plate, each time raising a tiny burr next to each pit left by the sharp points of the serrated edge. Rocking a plate can take hours, because it must be rocked completely in one direction, then at right angles to the first direction, then in the diagonal directions, and finally in the directions between the diagonals. See the diagram of rocking angles. At least eight rockings are necessary over the complete surface of the plate. Needless to say, the plate should be copper, because zinc will yield so many fewer impressions; and we assume that after all the work of rocking you will want an adequate edition.

When the plate is rocked to completion it will print as a solid black. The design is placed into the rough surface of the mezzotint by scraping and burnishing. Special knife scrapers and fine burnishers are available that make very delicate work possible. The rich quality of the blacks should be exploited, though, and it would be silly to scrape large areas of a mezzotint.

To do particularly small details it will be necessary to work in dark lines and tones with the point of a needle or a roulette wheel. Very small rockers made for detail work are helpful in reworking areas that have been overscraped. Roulettes are made in various sizes and in a number of patterns and textures. The irregular roulette is good for matching the texture of the rocked plate. In England a rocking apparatus is used to guide the rocker as it moves across the plate, making the lines parallel and easily controlled.

A deeply bitten aquatint will approximate but not equal the dense rich black of the mezzotint, and several artists have exploited this shortcut to good effect. During printing, the ink should be oilier than usual, and the plate hand-wiped. Use no paper wipe except for the highlights. Take as few proofs as possible during the working of the image. If a large edition is wanted, the copper may be steel-faced.

TRANSFERRING SKETCH TO PLATE

Carbon Paper

One of the most useful ways of placing a sketch in position on the plate is to redraw the essential lines on the grounded plate, using a carbon sheet made of chalk or pastel as a transfer paper. This paper may be made of white or yellow chalk smoothed evenly onto a piece of tracing paper or thin bond, and it may be used over and over again. Place the plate, hard-grounded and thoroughly dry, face up on the table, then position your sketch, face up, over the plate and tape the top corners to the table with masking tape. Put the chalked transfer paper between the sketch and plate, chalked side next to the ground. Then redraw only the main elements of the design, using a pencil or a blunted stylus. Do not press too heavily or you may damage the ground. Lift the papers to check your pressure after you have made a few strokes. Save your enthusiasm for the actual work with the needle when you start to draw through the ground. All the preliminary drawings mean nothing if you do not draw beautifully with the needle itself. The chalk transfer drawing will smudge rapidly unless you use a hand support to keep your hand off the plate while working.

Press Transfer

If you do your sketch on tracing paper or smooth bond paper with charcoal, carbon pencil, or soft lead pencil, it is possible to transfer the unfixed drawing directly on to the grounded plate by running both through the etching press. Reduce the pressure from the normal printing pressure, place the drawing, face down, in contact with the grounded plate, and pass it through the press. The ground must be hard, of course, and rough paper may cause enough of the ground to lift off to foul-bite the plate. This method automatically eliminates the need to reverse your drawing because your draw-

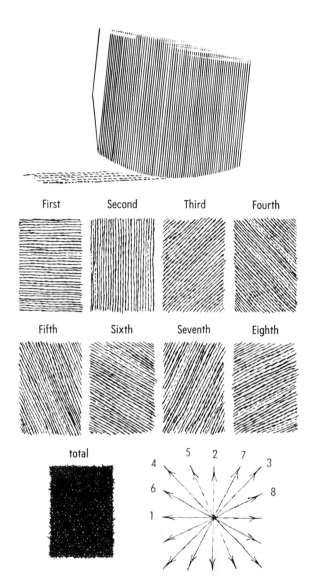

First   Second   Third   Fourth

Fifth   Sixth   Seventh   Eighth

total

MEZZOTINT CHART

Mario Avati creates his velvet blacks with a mezzotint rocker whose serrated edge produces countless tiny indentations and raised burrs into the surface of the copper plate. The handle is heavily taped to cushion the rocker for the time-consuming job.

The etched line of Kathe Kollwitz is revealed by the glistening of the ink as it lies on the paper.

The checkerboard effect is caused by a parallel line roulette, used in two directions at right angles to each other. Print by Ross.

Below: The central texture is caused by a parallel roulette on top of a fabric-textured soft-ground tone.

ing is reversed as it is transferred, then restored when it is printed from the plate.

ETCHING NEEDLES AND ROULETTES

Any point that will remove the ground will enable you to etch the resultant line in acid. Old dental tools are good, if resharpened to suit your hand. Commercially made etching needles, with a steel point set in a wooden, pencil-like handle, are also practical, if expensive. You can sharpen a nail, if you wish, as long as you can draw fluently with it. However, an overly sharp point may catch in the metal and stick. Because the line will not bite if all the wax is not removed from the line, a very light touch is somewhat dangerous.

Various roulette wheels are made in order to produce a variety of tones and patterns in the plate. They can provide regular patterns, usually numbered according to the number of lines or dots per inch that are incised into the drum, and irregular patterns, which are usually handmade. Roulettes are expensive but very helpful when different textures and tones are needed. They can be used to cut directly into the metal of the plate, when the tones will print dark from the burr produced by the tiny metal edges. Roulettes may be used with ground, and the textures will be bitten deeply and permanently into the plate by the acid. Linear roulettes will produce continuous parallel lines if the tool is rolled back and forth without slipping or skidding.

Old phonograph needles, pins stuck into erasers, sticks, punches, and all sorts of implements have been used to make lines or textures in etching, and you will have to decide which points best serve your purpose.

ACIDS

Nitric (For Etching Zinc and Copper)

One of the most useful acids is nitric; it will etch either zinc or copper. When purchased in technical grade, it is very strong and quite dangerous and should be handled with care. It is not necessary to buy the chemically pure acid for etching. It is mixed with water to various dilutions; the stronger solutions, such as 4 parts water to one part nitric, usually used for deep biting or strong line work and the weak solutions, such as 8 or 12 parts water to one part nitric, usually used for aquatints and fine lines.

When diluting acid, always put the water into the container first, then add the acid. Use a glass measuring cup and work slowly and carefully. Never leave acid where it can accidentally be knocked over. Put it away in a locked cabinet when you are not using it.

Zinc plates will release white bubbles of hydrogen gas in nitric acid, which will indicate the strength of the acid. Intense bubbling shows a fresh, strong acid and faint bubbling results from weak or exhausted acid. Nitric acid biting into zinc produces a rugged, irregular line if the plate is left too long in the acid. It is advisable to keep a bottle of ammonia handy, in case of acid splashed on clothing, to neutralize the action of the acid with the base. Because a drop of acid will eat a hole in clothing very rapidly, work aprons or old clothes are essential in the shop.

Dutch Mordant (For Etching Copper)

The standard formula for Dutch mordant, for etching copper, is:

Hydrochloric acid	10%
Potassium chlorate	2%
Water	88%

Dissolve the potassium chlorate in water first, then add the hydrochloric acid. This acid, used for copper plates, bites slowly and is wonderful for fine lines and aquatints because it is easy to control the depth of the bite. As no bubbles are produced, careful observation of the solution's action is necessary. Dutch mordant is favored by artists who want good control over even, close tones and who want no accidental effects or textures. Be sure to label all your acid solutions clearly. The mordant turns greenish-blue after its first use and is easy to identify but should be labeled as a matter of policy of good housekeeping. Proper organization is essential to success in most endeavors, and printmaking demands all the organizational skill you can muster.

Ferric Chloride (For Etching Copper)

Ferric chloride (iron perchloride) acid, long used by commercial photoengravers, is able to bite copper plates with precision and is useful for fine work and aquatints. It bites very slowly, and plates should be turned face down in the solution to allow the precipitate to fall out of the lines, where it would eventually clog them if left to accumulate. This method prevents visual observation while the plate is biting and mandates an accurate timing procedure, which some artists resent, and therefore they reject the acid. It is usually diluted with equal amounts of water to make a reddish-brown solution. If you can establish a reliable timing chart, ferric chloride should be extremely useful.

Aluminum Etch

While aluminum is too soft for general work, it is cheaper than zinc or copper, and some beginning students may find it helpful for experimental work in elementary techniques. An acid to etch aluminum can be made by mixing the following chemicals into ten parts of warm water: one part potassium dichlorate, one part sulphuric acid and one and one-half parts of hydrochloric acid. All these chemicals are mixed by weight, not volume.

Acid Trays

For plates up to 30″ by 24″ it is possible to buy photo trays made of a white plastic material that successfully resists acids. These trays are readily available and are not expensive. Black rubber photographic trays may also be used, but they disintegrate in time and are not as durable as the white plastic. Stainless steel trays are best of all because they are

An irregular roulette with a carbide tip will roughen the surface of a plate into a deep black, if desired. The tone produced is close to a mezzotint black in effect.

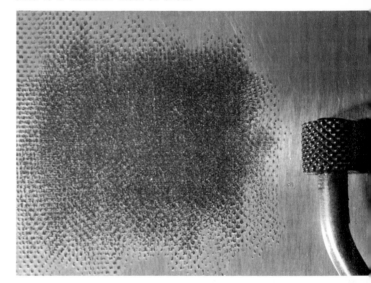

A regular roulette produces a more mechanical tone than the irregular tip. They are made in a number of patterns and sizes.

A lining roulette will make parallel lines that form an even tone. They may be cross-hatched by holding the tool at a right angle to the first set of lines.

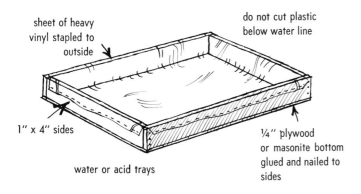

sheet of heavy vinyl stapled to outside

do not cut plastic below water line

1" x 4" sides

¼" plywood or masonite bottom glued and nailed to sides

water or acid trays

CHEAP LARGE WATER OR ACID TRAY

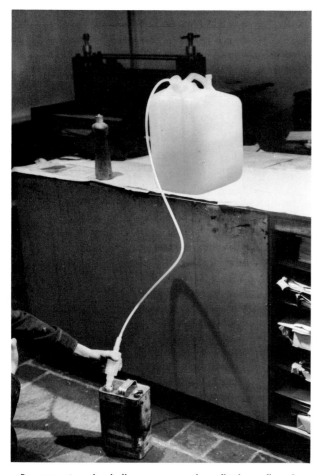

By squeezing the bulb, you can induce fluids to flow from the large storage container to the smaller can. This type of siphon is very useful in the graphic workshop for draining acid trays and transferring liquids without spillage.

Below: The plate should be eased into the acid tray. It should be lifted on end every minute or so in order to remove gas bubbles. Do not brush a soft-ground to remove bubbles.

strong and unbreakable, but they are quite expensive. For larger plates you may have to order custom-made plastic trays from a photo supply house. Lacquer thinner will dissolve some photographic trays, and care must be taken to test the tray first in order to avoid softening the surface when you use this solvent.

It is easy to make trays from pieces of 1" by 4" pine, with a bottom of ¼" plywood or ¼" hardboard. While it is possible to waterproof this type of tray with tapes and varnishes, the easiest way to make it usable is to line the inside of the tray with vinyl or plastic sheeting, folded up over the sides and stapled to the outside of the 1" by 4" framework. This lining will make the tray suitable for water and all acids, and any size desired may be constructed quickly and cheaply. The plastic sheeting may be replaced rapidly, as it tends to develop pinholes and tears, particularly if the plates have sharp edges. We have used many trays of this type and find them easy to maintain and inexpensive.

Emptying Acid Trays

The most convenient way to drain acid from a tray is from a spigot built into the bottom. This type of tray is very expensive, however, and few artists can afford them. A useful substitute is a hand-pumped siphon that operates on gravity, once the siphoning process has been started. Most of the siphons are available from automobile accessory stores and were designed to siphon gasoline and similar fluids. They are made from white plastic, which is acid-proof, and have ¼"-diameter plastic hoses. They will drain a gallon of liquid in about 5 minutes, which is the major disadvantage of the method, because the time involved seems excessively long when you are cleaning up the workshop. However, there is no danger of spilling the acid, which is important enough to make the wait worthwhile. The siphon can also be used to transfer varnoline, lacquer thinner, and other fluids from one container to another.

Small quantities of acid can be poured into a funnel set in the mouth of the container. Plastic containers are useful but occasionally develop leaks, and glass bottles are breakable but never leak. Acid bottles should have plastic caps or ground-glass stoppers. Metal caps will soon corrode through from the fumes in the bottle.

Biting the Plate

Plates should be eased into the acid bath to avoid splashing or spilling the solution. A hooked dental tool makes a convenient implement with which to hold the plate while it is being immersed in the acid. Be careful not to scratch the ground. Examine the plate after a few moments to see if the lines are all biting correctly, or if any areas are false-biting. A false bite will occur in a section of plate where the ground has been bruised or damaged in a way hard to detect. Remove the plate promptly and stop out the offending areas with a stop-out varnish, such as rosin dissolved in alcohol, shellac, or even liquid hard ground.

If the acid is nitric, gas bubbles will soon form in the lines. Bubbles should be removed by lifting one edge of the plate out of the acid with a hook and letting all the acid drain off the surface. Then replace the plate in the solution. Bubbles should be removed regularly to avoid an irregular, ragged line, unless this effect is desired. The traditional turkey feather to remove bubbles is still used, and as long as it does not scratch the ground is a helpful tool, though somewhat inefficient. With soft grounds, it is not possible to brush the plate with anything because of the danger of scratching the ground. These plates must be lifted and drained.

Drawing on the Immersed Plate

If certain lines are not biting properly, it is possible to work on the plate while it is still in the acid bath. You must remember that the longer the lines bite, the deeper and darker they get. This means that all delicate work should be done last and heavier lines should be needled in as soon as possible. Francis Seymour Haden, a 19th century English etcher, frequently worked on his plates while they were still in the acid. Good needles will corrode rapidly with this treatment, but resharpened dental tools will work admirably for this process.

Deep Biting

For relief etching where two thirds of the thickness of the plate must be removed, nitric acid is the strongest mordant and therefore the fastest. Because of the heat generated by the acid in removing large quantities of metal, it is wise to have a second tray containing cold water alongside the acid tray. When the plate becomes warm, slide it into the water for a minute or two to cool it. If the plate becomes too warm, the ground will become soft and, as the biting increases in vigor with heat, the whole process may escalate out of control and the plate be ruined by false biting and unwanted corrosion. Acid quickly loses its strength when deep biting of large areas is necessary, and the solution must be replenished frequently. Have plenty of ventilation for this procedure because the fumes are noxious. If much biting is done it should be in an area that has mechanical ventilation, with an outside vent. As the fumes are corrosive, most metal nearby will soon rust unless lacquered or otherwise protected.

Plates from photoengravers' supply houses are usually back-coated to protect the reverse side. Scratches and nicks are frequent, however, and if not protected will soon become very deep and, in rare cases, bitten through the plate. Check the backs of the plates being bitten deeply and retouch scratches with asphaltum or stop-out varnish.

DRYPOINT

Although this process may be the simplest in theory, it is quite difficult to control the drypoint technique when you need delicate drawing and even tonalities. The idea of using a sharp hard steel point to scratch into the plate is very appealing because it seems so simple and basic. However, etching is actually easier for the beginner to master, while the drypoint requires a high degree of skill. The burr of metal

When space is at a premium, water and acid trays may be stacked one above the other. Water must be on top, acid underneath. This setup is from the Graphic Art USA Exhibit in Belgrade, Yugoslavia, 1965. Trays have built-in spigots for easy draining.

Vented acid chamber in the studio of Rudy Pozzatti, Bloomington, Indiana. Note black siphon on left wall for draining solutions back into containers.

The single dry point needle scratches the plate, throwing up burr on one or both sides of the line, depending upon the angle of cut. The angle shown produces a double burr.

When inked, the dry point burr traps and holds a large amount of ink, printing the velvety black line so prized by dry point connoisseurs.

that is raised by the point actually holds more ink and prints with more effect than the incised line itself, which is usually quite shallow and holds little ink. When the burr is new, the print has rich, dark blacks; but when the burr starts to break off and wear down, the blacks get weaker and greyer until the plate has lost much of its character and vigor. A drypoint on zinc will yield only 25 or 30 impressions. Copper will furnish about double that number and, when steel-faced, may yield from 100 to 200 decent impressions. Hardened steel, carbide tips, and diamond points are all suitable for making dry-points. Lovis Cornith, Jacques Villon, and Max Beckmann have produced striking prints with this method.

CORRECTING ERRORS

Scraping, Burnishing, and Polishing

It is almost inevitable that some lines or tones will need to be eliminated or reduced in value. The scraper, a three-sided wedge of hardened steel, is the tool usually used for this job. It should be kept very sharp on a fine india or hard arkansas stone, and the steel shaft can be wrapped with masking tape to protect your fingers. Scrapers come in many sizes and shapes and are virtually indispensable to the etcher. Some methods, such as the mezzotint, rely exclusively on the scraper for the development of the image, while almost all techniques have some need for this useful tool. It can remove amounts of zinc or copper by scraping, and it acts as an eraser.

Lovis Corinth
"Selbstbildnis"
Drypoint 7¾" x 6⅛"
Metropolitan Museum of Art
Gift of Mr. and Bruno Adriani 1959

When working over a large area, use enough pressure and keep changing the angle of cut, in order to avoid building up ridges or "drifts," which are minute corrugations in the surface of the plate. A dull tool will add scratches instead of removing them, so keep the scraper sharp. The edge does the cutting; and as there are usually three edges to each tool, you can remove a lot of metal in a short time. You must scrape over an area and not just along a thin line or the scraped indentation will print as a grey smudge.

After the scraping is finished, the surface of the plate will have to be smoothed further, with fine sandpaper, such as 0000 or finer. This surface, in turn, would print as a smoky grey tone and will have to be burnished and charcoaled for a smooth polish. It may be necessary to use jeweler's rouge for the final polishing if a brilliant white is desired. Engraver's charcoal, made from hard maple, is usually used with water to increase its efficiency. A few drops sprinkled on the area to be polished will be sufficient. Without water, charcoal does not cut as well.

Repoussage

If the plate has been scraped to such an extent that the surface is simply too low to print properly, it may be necessary to force the metal back to the original level from the back of the plate. This raising, called *repoussage*, may be done in several ways.

Mark the back of the plate with crayon or chalk outlining the area to be raised, using two pieces of wood fastened together as a caliper. You must have a smooth metal sheet as an anvil upon which to place the plate, face down. With a ball-peen hammer, hammer the back of the plate to force the metal up to the level of the printing surface. Hammer gently at first. The surface may then be sanded and polished until it is smooth and even again.

It is possible to glue paper shims on the back of the plate, in position, under the scraped area. Run the plate and shims through the etching press several times with enough pressure to force the metal up to required level. In fact, whichever method you use to force the metal to the correct level, it is a good idea to glue paper shims on the back of the plate to prevent the scraped area from being pushed down again by repeated printings under strong pressure.

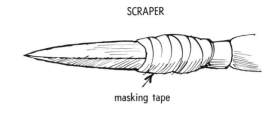

SCRAPER

masking tape

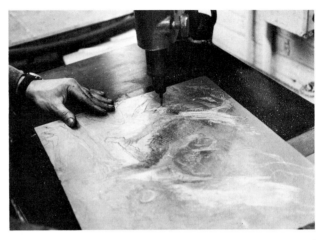

Al Blaustein uses a photoengraver's router to remove unwanted lines from a zinc plate. The router is locked into position and the plate is tilted slightly to control the depth of cut. Pratt Institute, Brooklyn.

Minor scratches may be removed by polishing the plate with engraver's charcoal and water.

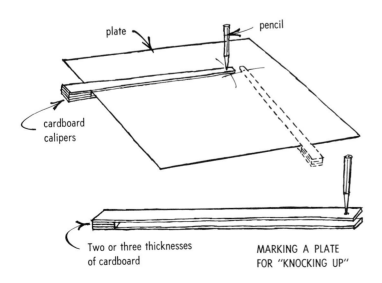

plate

pencil

cardboard calipers

Two or three thicknesses of cardboard

MARKING A PLATE FOR "KNOCKING UP"

PAPER

Etchings are printed into damp paper because the fibers must be soft and pliant in order to be pressed into the incisions and indentations of the metal plate. The ability of the paper to withstand the abuse of printing, dampening, pressure, and stretching without tearing or discoloring is of primary importance. Most highly prized papers are made of all rags, with little sizing, long fibers, and no chemical residue. Good papers come from Europe and Japan, with France, Italy, and Germany still the prime producers of rag base papers suitable for intaglio printing.

Proof Paper

Good proof impressions can be taken on index paper, cover stock, Basingwerk, or other papers that will not disintegrate when they are dampened. It is possible to use newsprint for a rough proof, but it is so soft that it tears easily and of course it is extremely perishable. For a finished proof it is wise to use the paper on which you will print the entire edition, in order to judge the tonal values exactly as they appear in a final print. Proof papers need not be 100% rag because you are not concerned with the permanency of the proof, until the image is complete enough to warrant preservation.

Dampening Paper

The paper must be soaked in water to soften the fibers. Many papers can be completely immersed and left to soak. This should be done before you start the inking and wiping process.

Many papers may be soaked directly in a tray of water, then rolled between clean blotters until the surface moisture has been absorbed. A hard-rubber roller, plastic roller, or wooden rolling pin may be used to blot the excess moisture. Most papers need only a few minutes in the water bath to be ready to use. For proving plates and for small editions this method is satisfactory, but because rolling the paper between blotters is time consuming it is faster to prepare paper in advance when larger editions are needed.

The day before you print you can prepare a stack of paper, 20 or more sheets, by dampening every other sheet with a moist sponge. Stack the sheets together and wrap them in vinyl or oilcloth, and the moisture will be distributed evenly throughout the stack in 24 hours. Make sure the sides are covered or they will dry first. The amount of water needed depends on the absorbency of the particular paper, which can be determined only by experience. Some notes on popular papers follow.

Domestic Papers

Strathmore makes an all-rag paper suitable for etchings, called Artist's paper. It is expensive but strong and fine. Acme Index and Beckett cover papers have a rag content and print well for inexpensive papers. Tweedweave, Alexandra, Pastelle, Hammermill, and Tuscan are machine-made papers of fair quality, suitable for proofs and student work.

Imported Papers

Rives, light and heavy, is a standard paper, all rag, good quality, and suitable for many plates.

Rives BFK, a heavy, fine paper, is available in many sizes.

It is a very useful paper for etchings, collagraphs, and lithographs and has become one of the most respected papers made.

Arches text, available in buff and white, both laid and wove, is a rag paper used extensively in this country and Europe. It is good for small plates and plates that are not too deeply bitten.

Arches cover is a fine, heavy, sensitive paper useful for collagraphs, etchings, and lithos. The buff color is very handsome.

Basingwerk, made in three weights, is a useful paper for proofs and for some editions. It is inexpensive and practical.

Fabriano Classico, in various weights up to 300 lb., is a watercolor paper. The heavier paper is very strong and suitable for embossing, collagraphs, and deeply bitten plates. The deckle edge is worth saving. An expensive sheet.

Copperplate is a fine paper, but it can not be soaked as it falls apart if too wet. Should be dampened by blotters only and handled carefully.

Fabriano text and cover is available in many beautiful colors and is one of the few colored papers that may be used for etching. It is not an all-rag sheet.

German etching paper is a good, large white sheet, moderately expensive and fairly useful.

Italia is white, strong, good for etching, collagraphs and general intaglio printing. A paper well liked by many printmakers, it is moderately expensive.

J. Barcham Green watercolor paper is a nice sheet, good sized and well made. It is a standard paper in England and deservedly so.

Millbourn is available in many weights, and the heavier sheets are a joy to hold and very expensive to buy. Use it for special plates.

Murillo is a light buff color, very heavy, marvelous for collagraphs and extraordinarily sensitive for black-and-white etchings. If this paper were made in white it would be one of the most popular sheets around.

Umbria is a good, useful paper in a medium size sheet.

Kochi, a Japanese paper, is suitable for etching if not soaked, but merely dampened.

Oldrich Kulhanek
(Czechoslovakia)
"Make-up" 1968
Etching 15¾" x 11"
Courtesy of the artist

Dampening Trays

For small sheets of paper the standard size photo-trays made of white plastic are suitable. Larger sheets may need a tray made to fit. The construction may follow the directions for acid trays, using 1" by 4" lumber and a plywood or pressed wood bottom, covered with a sheet of heavy vinyl. The most convenient tray has a spigot built in to allow easy drainage. Paper left in trays will form slime and mildew after a few days. The odor generated from this mess can be highly unpleasant, so keep your water trays clean by regular rinsing. A few drops of household bleach added to the water will keep mold to a minimum.

ETCHING INK

The chemical components of etching ink are very simple, and it is relatively easy to make your own. Linseed oil, the

Used army-surplus mixer used for mixing pigment and plate oil in ink manufacture at Indiana University.

Inking the etched plate with a cardboard squeegee is a fast, efficient method for normally bitten plates.

basic ingredient, is added to powdered pigment, and this mixture makes etching ink. There are several brands of ink commercially available, some very inexpensive and of good quality. It is usually sold in 1-pound cans, and the waxed-paper lid should be carefully replaced on the ink before the lid is put on the can after each use. It is more important to put the paper disc on the ink, with no air bubbles underneath, than to put the metal lid on the can. If the ink hardens over, it is messy and wasteful to skim off the top to reach the fresh ink underneath. If you make your own ink, it should be preserved in cans or jars with a similar paper disc as a seal against air.

There are several black pigments available that will make good ink, such as bone black, Frankfort black, vine black, lamp black, ivory black, and drop black. They can be mixed together to exploit the best characteristics of each. One pigment does not have all the qualities essential to good ink, such as intensity and strength of color, even texture, and easy wiping. Mars black is normally not suitable for etching ink. The addition of umber or ochre or blue will make the ink take on warm or cool tones as it is wiped. Mix the dry powdered pigments first with a palette knife, then add a small quantity of plate oil, which is thickened linseed oil. A grinding muller is used for small quantities of ink, with an old litho stone or a glass or marble slab as a grinding surface.

Rudy Pozzatti, of Indiana University, suggests the following ink formulas:

For general printing	3 parts vine black
	1 part bone black
For printing drypoints	4 to 6 parts vine black
	1 part bone black
For printing engravings	2 parts vine black
	1 part bone black

When very large quantities of ink are needed, some schools use power mixers to combine the pigment and oil. The University of Indiana has a used dough-mixing machine in which it mixes the basic ingredients. Power mixers are economically feasible only when hundreds of pounds of ink are needed, to offset the initial cost of the equipment.

The thickened linseed oil that must be used in ink-making can be purchased as plate oil or be made by boiling raw linseed oil until it thickens. Linseed oil may also be thickened by lighting a match to the surface and burning off excess fluids, a smelly and somewhat dangerous procedure. If the oil is not thickened, the ink made from it is difficult to wipe and prints weakly. Most printers buy their ink from reputable manufacturers.

Inking the Plate

The ink must be forced into the etched or engraved lines, the surface wiped clean, and the plate printed onto dampened paper through the etching press. There are several methods of applying the ink.

Inking with Cards

A very quick and easy way to ink a plate, and to accomplish a good part of the wiping, is to use small matboard or chipboard rectangles of cardboard, about 3″ by 4″, as small squeegees, to push the ink over the surface of the plate and into the lines. The edges of the cards must be cut straight and smooth. A good papercutter will be the most useful tool for cutting. Cut the boards into long strips 3″ or 4″ wide, then cut one or two strips at a time into the rectangles that you need. The inking is very fast and the first wiping even faster with these cards. You will save a great amount of tarletan or crinoline by the use of the cards because most of the excess ink will be removed before you start the rag-wiping. The disposable cards are made from scrap pieces of matboard. A rubber window-cleaning squeegee is handy. It can be cleaned with a rag and used instead of cards.

Inking with a Roller

Small paint rollers, 3″ to 6″ in length, are good for distributing the ink over the plate and for getting the ink into the lines. Mohair and short-nap rollers are easiest to clean and are preferred, but almost any nap is usable. The problem comes when you have to clean the roller after you have used it. If it isn't cleaned it soon hardens into a rocklike cylinder and is more trouble to clean than it's worth.

Inking with a Dabber

Rolled scraps of blanket felt make good dabbers, useful for pushing ink into the incised lines of an etching plate. The felt strip should be from 5″ to 8″ in width and 20 or more inches in length. Roll it tightly, and use string, masking tape, or rubber bands to hold it in place. Cut the ends smooth with a hacksaw or sharp knife, and keep cutting new felt as the ends harden. Dried ink is a distinct handicap to the dabber, which is useful mainly for small plates or for spots that have been missed with the card or roller. Leather dabbers are used, too, and they are easier to clean and to keep soft and supple. They are made somewhat differently than felt dabbers, being filled with cotton waste or an old soft rag and then tied with string into a shape that makes a good handle.

Inking the etched plate with a pad of crinoline. Atelier Desjobert, Paris.

Inking is accomplished in this intaglio print workshop with a roller.

Below: Inking the etched plate with a dabber made of old etching felts. This procedure is useful for very deeply bitten plates.

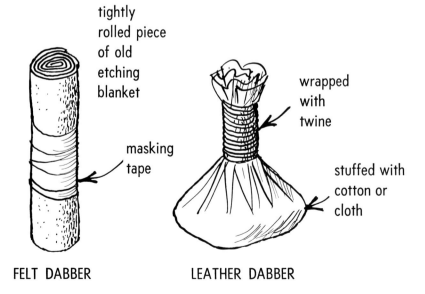

tightly
rolled piece
of old
etching
blanket

masking
tape

FELT DABBER

wrapped
with
twine

stuffed with
cotton or
cloth

LEATHER DABBER

Custom-made hotplate built in on level with table top. Indiana University.

Commercial restaurant hotplate that has been found serviceable by Indiana University.

Inexpensive two-burner electric hotplate with open grid surface. This type heats the plate quickly but does not retain heat long. Indiana University.

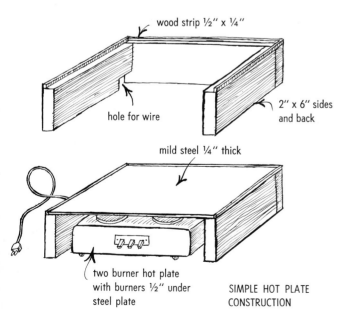

wood strip ½" x ¼"

hole for wire

2" x 6" sides and back

mild steel ¼" thick

two burner hot plate with burners ½" under steel plate

SIMPLE HOT PLATE CONSTRUCTION

Gloves

When you are inking large plates or printing a big edition it is helpful to wear cotton work gloves; the problem of inky hands is ever present in the workshop, and gloves keep at least part of the ink away. The hardware store sells cotton work gloves with knit cuffs, and these are best. Rubber or vinyl gloves make your hands sweat and are uncomfortable after a few prints. The gauntlet type of glove is too awkward. Leather gloves are good if you have an old pair that you won't mind soiling. The gloves must be removed for hand wiping and for paper handling.

Hotplates

The hotplate is essential in the etcher's studio, not only for fusing rosin aquatints to the plate but for warming those plates that need very rich and full printing to bring out their best characteristics. Most professional etching printers rarely use the hotplate in printing plates, however, because it may cause more problems than it solves. In general, ink at room temperature, if wiped when fresh and not left to dry out, will yield good prints, particularly from plates that are normally bitten and not worn. Problems that arise from use of the hotplate are these:

1. If the plate is overheated it may bake the ink into the finer lines, causing them to print faintly.

2. The plate will develop a buckle in the center if it is heated too much. Sometimes this fault comes out when the plate is cooled, but sometimes it does not.

3. If the plate is printed when it is too hot, it may dry the paper somewhat and cause spotty effects. The heat dries the paper quickly, in any case, so that multiple-plate color printing is difficult to register when the second plates are being printed.

However, it is undeniable that slight warming does enrich a weak plate and enhance tonality. Learn to be judicious in your printing, and use the hotplate with care. It certainly is necessary in a cold workshop.

The best hotplates are made commercially, usually for restaurant kitchens where quantity frying is done, but these are very expensive unless purchased from a dealer in used kitchen equipment. A good hotplate can be made from a two-burner electric heater of excellent quality. Arrange a piece of ¼"-thick steel plate on a frame of wood or angle-iron so that the electric heater can slide underneath and almost touch the underside of the steel plate. You can shim up the heater with asbestos or other fire-resistant material. The area of the steel plate should be large enough to accommodate your larger plates and should have a flush top surface with no screws or nails sticking up to damage your plates.

Although many older workshops had gas-flame hotplates (even wood charcoal has been used) it seems silly, these days, to tolerate the dangers of an open flame in such a promising place for a fire as a printmaker's workshop. We have used the kitchen gas range when speed and high heat was desirable, but it is more prudent to rely on electric heat and check the wiring frequently!

Wiping the Plate

The initial wiping of the inked plate should be done with tarletan or crinoline, which is somewhat like starched cheesecloth. It should be balled into a mass that fits the hand comfortably. You can wipe, with light pressure, in a circular manner or in one direction after another. The purpose of wiping is to remove most of the ink from the surface of the plate while still leaving it in the etched lines. At a certain point, when the design is visible but somewhat hazy or smoky, the rag wiping should be stopped. If the plate is overwiped the lines will be weak or broken and tonal values will be dry or light. A little oil of cloves added to the ink beforehand will prevent quick drying and lengthen the time you can spend on the wiping.

Hand Wiping

At the point when the etching design is still slightly blurred, the hand wiping should start. If too much ink still remains on the plate, it will not wipe clean, as it should after a few strokes with the edge of the palm. Use the side of your palm, and wipe quickly, with very light pressure, over the surface of the plate. Copper wipes faster than zinc. Plates with large amounts of white area are more difficult to wipe than darker, more tonal plates, because more ink must be removed from the surface. Wipe thoroughly, removing all the smears and surface blurs. Wipe your hand frequently on a cloth or on some newspaper kept nearby. You cannot clean wipe a plate with dirty hands. Work quickly and efficiently. If you wait too long before printing the plate the ink will start to dry and the print will be weak and pale.

Paper Wiping

With some plates, newsprint or pages from old telephone books can be used to wipe the ink from the surface, instead of hand wiping. The paper polishes the metal and makes for a brilliant print with whiter whites than the hand can produce. Too much paper wiping, however, will overwipe the plate. In general, aquatint tones will be richer if hand wiped only. Those areas of the plate which are white or very light can be lightly paper-wiped just before printing. Do not use paper towels or tissues to wipe because they are too absorbent and pull too much ink from the etched lines. Wiping plates is somewhat tricky and a little practice is necessary to achieve good results. However, no magic touch is necessary. We have taught students to ink, wipe, and print plates in a professional manner in a very short time. Roughly bitten plates, collagraphs, and materials other than copper or zinc are more difficult to print, however, and some experience is desirable to get the best results from printing these kinds of plates. Don't forget to wipe the edges of your plate, too. The plate must now be printed promptly.

PREPARING TO PRINT

Placing the Plate on the Bed

The bed of the press should be run out to one side of the press. Put clean newsprint on the bed to keep your impres-

After wiping with the cards, crinoline or tarletan rag is used to wipe, in a circular motion with little pressure. When the image is fairly clear, but still a little smoky or hazy, stop wiping with the rag. Too much rag wiping will weaken the lines.

The hand wipe is accomplished with a light, fast stroke, using the side of the palm. A few strokes in one spot should brighten the area and wipe the surface clean.

Below: The paper wipe, if used, will polish the surface even more than the hand, and will give a more brilliant plate tone. Some plates need paper wiping more than others. To keep rich aquatint tones, use a minimum of paper wiping.

The freshly inked plate is placed, face up, on the bed of the etching press. The bed is lined with clean newsprint to keep the margins of your print clean. Once the plate is down, do not move it, as smudges on the newsprint will print.

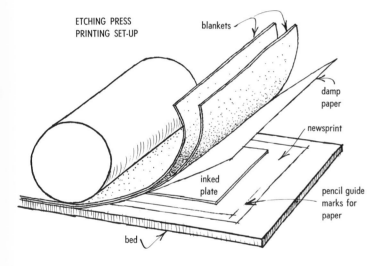

ETCHING PRESS PRINTING SET-UP

blankets

damp paper

newsprint

inked plate

pencil guide marks for paper

bed

sion paper clean. A print can be ruined by smudges of ink in the image or in the margins. Some printers tape a sheet of heavy acetate over the newsprint and keep this surface clean with rags or paper towels. In any case, the bed of the press should be clean and free of dirt, dust, or particles of any kind.

Now place the freshly inked and wiped plate on the clean bed, inked side up. Put it down without sliding or moving it after it touches the bed. Some printers wipe the back of the plate because ink always appears there. If you move the plate you may create smudges on the clean bed, and they could print.

Blotting the Paper

Pick up your paper from the water tray, using paper picks or fingers to keep the edges clean. Let the sheet drain for a minute or two into the tray, then place it between two clean white blotters. Using a rolling pin or a hard plastic roller, blot the excess water from the surface of your paper. If you are not using a water tray but are taking the paper from a stack of dampened sheets it need not be placed between blotters but can be put directly on the plate. Hold the paper with the paper picks by diagonally opposite corners for the most control in handling the sheet. Place the paper on top of the plate, centering it to obtain even margins. If you want consistent margins in edition printing you should mark the newsprint paper to note the positions of one side and one corner. Mark it before printing. Smooth the blankets over the paper. Some printers place a clean piece of newsprint between the back of the dampened paper and the blankets, but this is necessary only if your blankets are dirty or your paper is so thin that there is a danger of the ink coming through to stain the blankets.

Etching Blankets

The printing blankets normally used in the etching press are made of woven woolen felt. They are available in several

Left: Pick up the dampened paper with "picks" made of stiff, folded paper.
Right: Remove the paper from the water tray. Let the bulk of the water drain back into the tray before placing the paper between blotters to remove excess moisture.

Alfred Blaustein
"The Presentation" 1971
Etching 14⅜" x 17¾"
Courtesy of the artist

thicknesses, from around ¹⁄₁₆" to ³⁄₁₆". As they are usually
sold by weight (at $5.00 or more per pound) a set of two
or three blankets for a 24" by 48" bed size will cost from
$25 to $30. They can be washed in Woolite or a mild detergent every time they become stiff from the accumulation
of dried sizing from continuous printing. To dry woolen
blankets, pin or nail them to size to prevent shrinkage. They
can be washed in a bathtub or large sink and can be pinned
to a wall, a table, or a piece of plywood. Steel nails will rust.
Thin aluminum nails are best. Although woven felt is best
in the long run because of its fine even texture and its ability
to withstand hard wear, it is cheaper to buy pressed felt
blankets, which cost less than half the price. The pressed
felt is available in white and grey and in many thicknesses.
It is coarser in texture and is not always suitable for fine
even aquatints or large areas of even tone which may appear
mottled or blotchy. Pressed felt is good for roughly bitten
plates or collagraphs. A 1"-thick foam rubber slab can be
used as a blanket for collagraphs or in conjunction with a
blanket. The foam breaks up quickly and, unless it is handled
carefully, has a very short life. In an emergency ordinary
colored felt can be used, as can three or four new blotters,

which will print etchings if they are not too deeply bitten. Do not leave blankets in the press overnight. They get damp from contact with the printing paper and can rust the rollers and the bed with continued contact. Hang the blankets over a wooden bar or roll them up and put them away. The blankets should be cut to the width of the roller and somewhat shorter than the length of the bed. They should be aligned carefully to square with the bed. Crooked blankets will get caught in the press and the corners will be cut or torn, a common sight in print workshops with many beginning printmakers. Some workshops demand that each student provide his own blankets!

THE ETCHING PRESS

So many presses are being made at this time that we have prepared a chart showing the manufacturer's name and address, the size of press he makes, the cost, and other information and comments that seem appropriate. Used presses are scarce, although they should be coming on the market as the total quantity of presses increases. Old ungeared presses turn up now and then, but they should be checked for worn bearings or bushings. Beds tend to warp, too, and should be checked with a straightedge. Warps of more than $\frac{1}{16}$" in the center may cause trouble.

The basic etching press is a steel or Benelux bed, which passes between two steel rollers. There are usually guides to keep the bed from moving out of position or from falling off the end of the press. Small presses may be ungeared, but presses with beds wider than 18" should be geared. Chain-drive presses are very common because they can have high gear ratios, making possible the easy printing of deeply bitten plates, which need great pressure. Planetary-gear presses are good but require more physical effort than the worm-gear presses. Some of the better presses are made by Charles Brand, Graphic Chemical, Rembrandt Graphic Arts, Meeker-McFee, Glen Alps, American French Tool Co., and Wilfred Kimber. Check with the manufacturer for the latest prices; they have been going up constantly over the past few years.

Motorized presses are made by many companies because of the demand for large presses. It is a difficult job to print large plates by hand unless the gearing system is very efficient. Our own press is a 30" by 50" motorized Brand that has worked well for five years. Micrometer gauges are a big help when plates of different thicknesses are to be printed or when blankets are frequently changed. They are essential in a school or workshop with many students. Without micrometers the adjusting screws have to be changed by trial and error, which results in a ruined print now and then. Pressure can also be adjusted by adding or removing blankets. A slight increase in pressure can be obtained by adding a blotter or two on top of the blankets before running the press.

PRINTING THE PLATE

The best prints are pulled from a freshly inked and wiped plate. Ink starts to dry in a few minutes, and nothing should be allowed to interfere with the printing cycle once it has been started. Run the plate through the press once. If the pressure has been properly set, one printing should be enough. Every time you double-print a plate (pass it through the press twice) you run the risk of a double image or a blurred print because of the slight shifting of the paper. It will shift if the lines are not deeply bitten or if the paper dries and shrinks a little from contact with a warm plate. If you must adjust the pressure do it quickly so that the paper does not dry in the blankets. Loss of humidity causes the paper to shrink. Remove the proof by lifting the edge with paper picks. Pull the proof slowly enough to prevent tearing of the soft paper. Too much pressure will cause the print to be mashed into the plate, sometimes so tightly that it is impossible to save the print. If the plate curls, the pressure is too great. Run it through the press face down to straighten it out.

Run the plate, paper, and blankets through the press, once. The pressure should be enough to force the paper into all the etched lines, pulling the ink out of them and making the print, or proof, or impression from the plate.

Drying the Print

The usual methods of drying prints are simple but very important. A buckled or curled print will never fit properly in a mat or a frame. If you have excess margin on your paper you may tape the damp proof to a plywood board or a wall, using 1½"-wide gummed paper tape around all four edges. You may also staple the edges, about ¼" from the edge, placing the staples no more than 2" or 3" apart. The paper must be trimmed after the print is dry, which usually takes a day or less.

If you do not want to trim the paper or if you have a large number of prints to dry you can put them between blotters, with clean newsprint next to the fresh ink. Place transite or asbestos boards on top of every couple of prints to keep the weight on the prints. The blotters and newsprint should be changed every day until the prints are thoroughly dry. Drying can take from 2 to 5 days, depending on the thickness of the paper and the humidity of your studio. If you take prints out too soon they will buckle afterwards. The blotter method keeps the maximum embossment of the impression. The tape and the staple methods force the paper to shrink, flattening a good deal of the embossment. Remove the staples with the tip of a curved burnisher when the print is dry.

Typical plate-cleaning box, filled with sawdust saturated with varsol, varnoline, mineral spirits, or other low-volatility cleaning solvent. Indiana University.

Cleaning and Storing the Plate

Clean the plate with mineral spirits, varnoline, sub-turps or, if it is very dirty, with lacquer thinner. Coat the plate with asphaltum, heavy grease, or hard ground to keep it from rusting. If you are going to store the plate for a long time wrap it in wax paper first, then in newspaper or brown wrapping paper. Do not leave newsprint paper in prolonged contact with the plate, as the acid inherent in the paper will corrode the plate.

Intaglio Color Printing

Inking the plate a la poupeé (with small fabric "dolls"), each with a separate color. Colors may merge when areas are not defined by white spaces. Printed at Lacouriere's workshop in Paris.

Paolo Boni
"Germe"
Cut and riveted intaglio plate 17½" x 12⅞"
Associated American Artists Gallery

ONE-PLATE METHOD

An etching plate may be inked with several colors by applying the ink with cards or small dabbers to certain areas. The cards can wipe the areas fairly well without too much merging of the colors, but when the final wiping is accomplished a certain amount of blending and mixing of colors is inevitable. Wipe the lighter colors first and use a separate piece of tarletan for each color. When you come to the final wiping use clean pieces of newsprint or, if you are wiping with your hand, be careful to keep the darker colors from contaminating the lighter colors. It is possible to print somewhat consistent editions, although precisely similar impressions are virtually impossible with this method.

THE CUT-PLATE METHOD

If you cut a zinc, copper or collage plate with a jigsaw into sections, somewhat like a puzzle, each section can be inked and wiped with a different color etching ink, the parts put back together, and the reassembled plate printed. The plate may be cut into pieces by deep biting in the acid bath. This way success in printing a uniform edition is much more likely because the colors have much less chance of contact with each other. Frequently, however, there is a white line around many of the forms because the cut removes metal and these cuts can not hold ink; they therefore print with a white "river" or "thread." If this white line is utilized as part of the image, it can enhance the print.

Plates may be cut into pieces with a high-temperature cutting torch, acid, saws, thinner plates with tin-snips, or scissors. Cardboard or masonite plates can be cut with knives, razor blades, jeweler's saws, or jigsaws. Of course these plates can also be inked by the relief process as well as the intaglio method by using rollers or brayers and letterpress ink.

STENCIL COLOR PRINTING
ON A SINGLE PLATE

Color can be placed on an etching plate prior to printing by the stencil process, using cut paper or sheet metal as the stencils. In this process the color shapes must be planned

Opposite:
Rudy Pozzatti
"Apollo" 1970
Color Intaglio 35½" x 23½"
Courtesy of the artist

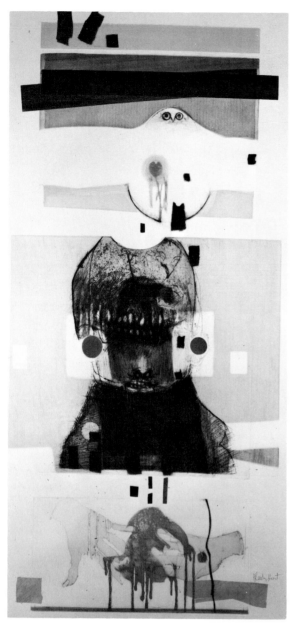

Mauricio Lasansky
"Bleeding Heart"
color intaglio 48¾" x 26"
Associated American Artists Gallery
Multiple plates overprinted.

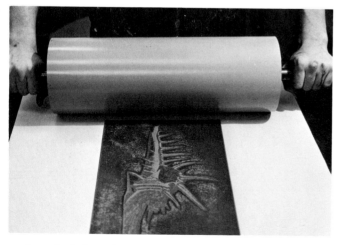

An etched plate which has been inked and wiped by the intaglio process is about to have its surface covered with a thin film of relief ink from a large composition roller. This roller should be large enough to cover the entire plate in one roll.

in advance and cut from acetate or an ink-resistant paper, such as tag or an oiled heavy bond paper. The shapes should be somewhat larger than actually wanted because the thickness of the paper hinders the roller from contact with the plate along the edge of the shape. A soft rubber or plastic roller can be used to roll the color on the plate. The procedure works best when executed in the following manner.

Cut the apertures in the stencil, using a razor blade or sharp knife. If you need overlapping colors, you must have separate stencils for each color. This practice is somewhat dangerous because the first color stenciled on the plate may be disturbed by the next stencil. Do not attempt too complicated a color-overlapping scheme. When your stencils are cut, mix the stencil color, using letterpress ink or etching color made less viscous than normal by the addition of linseed oil. The viscosity of the stenciled color must be less than that of the ink used for the intaglio lines in the plate. Now ink and wipe the plate with the basic etching ink, of normal or thick viscosity. Place the plate, face up, on a sheet of newsprint (acetate or glass is suitable) and position your first stencil over your inked etching plate. If you are printing an edition, you can tape the stencils in position and mark the position of the plate. On a separate inking slab, using a soft rubber or plastic roller, roll out a thin even film of the color to be stenciled on the plate. The roller should be large enough to cover the entire shape at one pass to avoid streaks. Be careful not to pull up the stencil, as it will tend to adhere to the ink on the roller. The ink deposit should be as perfect as possible to avoid having to go back and roll again. The first roll usually pulls up some intaglio color, which is transferred to the roller where it can contaminate the stencil color or be deposited back on the etching plate in the next pass of the roller. The plate may now be printed, in the usual manner, in the etching press. Because of the time involved in the inking process, it will be helpful to add oil of cloves to the etching ink to retard drying.

It is possible to add color to an etching impression that has dried. The stencil method may be used; but because the color will lie on top of the intaglio ink, it should be a thin transparent film unless it is to remain as a surface color, sitting on top of the intaglio impression. The stencil is placed directly on top of the paper and the color rolled on with soft rubber or plastic rollers. You may use water-based color for this technique, and as it sinks down into the paper and is naturally transparent it often works quite well. If too much color is deposited on the print, blot it off with clean newsprint.

SURFACE ROLLING

A surface color of letterpress ink may be rolled over an intaglio plate immediately prior to printing. The intaglio lines will stand out on top of the background color with clarity. The background film of ink must be thin and even, and a large roller, in perfect condition, is best for this purpose. Try to place the color on the plate with the least number of rolls to avoid pulling too much ink from the intaglio lines, weakening them and contaminating the color.

MULTIPLE-PLATE METHOD

To print intaglio plates in register is complicated by the fact that the dampened paper stretches as moisture is added. When printing two or more plates the shrinkage that occurs as the paper dries out causes problems in registering subsequent plates. Do not plan a register that will require precision that cannot be easily obtained by whatever method you employ. In general, color registry in the intaglio processes is not so accurate as that obtained in other procedures, such as silk screen, woodcut, and lithography. For this reason, many artists make mixed-media prints, trying to get the advantages of several processes in their images.

When you print from two or more plates in sequence, it is easier if the plates are of similar size and can be placed into a thin cardboard or heavy acetate mat taped to the bed of the etching press. This guide ensures that each plate is placed in precisely the same place each time. Cut the apertures carefully, avoiding making the opening too large, which would cause a shifting of the plates. The paper should have two straight sides and can easily be positioned by using folded masking-tape register tabs. Strapping tape, made of fibres, will make excellent register tabs. It is only necessary to have three tabs, two on one side and one on another side. Time is the enemy in this process, as the paper tends to dry out after the first printing while the second plate is being inked. If both plates are inked before printing, the ink on the first plate tends to dry. An efficient work setup makes the difference in color work! It is quite feasible to print an intaglio plate with several other colors on top of the first impression so that all the colors fuse and blend together in less than an hour. If the paper is kept damp between printings, the shrinkage will be minimized.

A rather primitive method of registering two plates consists of pulling a proof of the first plate, leaving the paper face up on a table, then placing the second plate, face down, directly over the impression of the first plate. The only difficulty with this method comes when you attempt to turn the plate and paper over in order to print it on the etching press. It takes good pressure with your hands to keep the paper from shifting as it is flipped over in contact with the plate. The process is useful for proofs and trying out various color combinations. Edition printing requires fixing the position of the plates with the mat method previously described.

COLOR BY TRANSFER FROM A ROLLER
TO AN INTAGLIO PLATE

You can transfer the design from any relief plate, such as a half-tone or a line photoengraving or a linoleum-cut block by taking the inked relief design on to the surface of a clean large plastic or composition roller in perfect condition. This image in turn, may be rolled over the surface of an inked intaglio plate, causing a combination of both images. The accompanying diagram indicates a procedure to keep the plates in proper register. The key to this process is the roller, which must be large enough to contain the entire image on its circumference. The guide strips can be made of

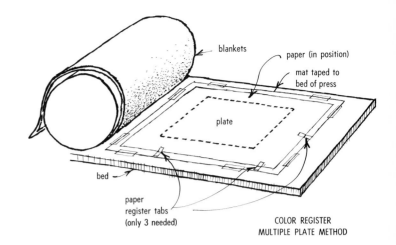

blankets
paper (in position)
mat taped to bed of press
plate
bed
paper register tabs (only 3 needed)

COLOR REGISTER MULTIPLE PLATE METHOD

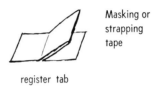

Masking or strapping tape

register tab

SCREEN PRINTING REGISTER TABS

Krishna Reddy
"Standing Woman"
Color Intaglio 17½" x 13½"
Associated American Artists Gallery
Printed by the viscosity method.

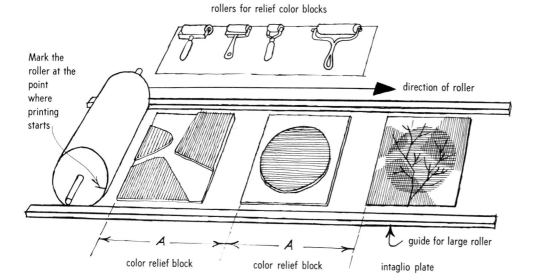

rollers for relief color blocks

Mark the roller at the point where printing starts

direction of roller

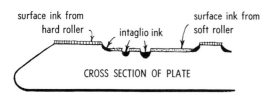

guide for large roller

A

A

color relief block

color relief block

intaglio plate

"A" equals circumference of large roller

surface ink from hard roller

intaglio ink

surface ink from soft roller

CROSS SECTION OF PLATE

To create multicolor prints from a combination of relief blocks and an intaglio plate, the intaglio plate should be inked and wiped first. Use oil of cloves in the ink to retard the drying time. Next ink the surface of the relief blocks with small brayers, using letterpress ink of less viscosity than the intaglio ink. Place the blocks and plate in the sequence shown, making sure that circumference of the large roller is adequate to carry the complete image. Mark the edge of the large roller at the point where the blocks start to print. At each complete turn of the roller the point where the next block should be placed will be clearly evident. Mark this point on your table so that the blocks will align properly in each printing cycle. As you roll the roller over each block, the color will be picked up on the roller and transferred to the intaglio plate at the end of the cycle. This plate should be printed promptly in the etching press, using dampened paper.

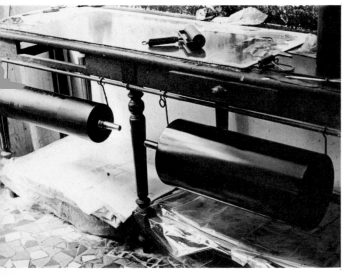

Large rollers are kept hanging from stiff wire brackets in Hayter's Atelier 17, Paris. The ink is applied to these rollers with a hand brayer, shown on the table top.

The large roller is spun by the left hand while the right hand moves the small brayer back and forth to distribute the ink evenly.

1" by 2" lumber stock, except when you use thick relief blocks, such as woodcuts, which may require 2" by 2" stock. The roller must be cleaned after each printing cycle. The etching plate must be inked and wiped each time, and in most cases, it must be cleaned, too, between inkings. Some remarkable juxtapositions of images are possible with this method.

MULTILEVEL COLOR INTAGLIO PRINTING

Stanley William Hayter has developed methods of printing which depend on varying levels in the plate, which can be inked with soft rollers and inks of different viscosities. These processes have enabled many artists to exploit textures and rhythms not obtainable by any other means. The method requires large rollers of varying hardnesses. The softest rollers will be pressed into the deepest levels, while the hardest rollers will touch only the highest levels of the plate.

The intaglio plate can be inked and wiped with the normal etching ink, of heavy viscosity as the first step in the process. A large, hard roller is then inked with an even film of loose non-viscous ink, such as letterpress ink mixed with enough linseed oil to make it very thin or soupy. This roller is passed over the plate with little pressure, inking only the highest parts of the plate. A second large roller, of softer material, such as gelatine or urethane, is now inked with an ink of medium viscosity and this roller is passed over the plate with heavy pressure to reach the lower levels. The highest levels which have been inked with the soupy ink will reject the stiffer ink. This system demands rollers in excellent condition because one pass of the roller should be enough to ink the plate. Rollers must be cleaned after each pass. Further information on color printing appears in the section on collagraphs.

CHINE COLLÉ

Chine Collé is another method for obtaining color in an etching through the use of colored paper collage. In this process, differently colored papers glued to the printing paper allow the artist to use flat color areas without two-plate printing. The colored paper can be cut or torn into shapes that will make a permanent part of the image. The pressure of the etching press will laminate the etching paper and the colored paper together with an adhesive such as dilute library paste or potato starch. When the etching plate is printed with intaglio methods, the lines and tones of the etched plate will print on top of the pasted paper forms.

Colored papers that may be used include Moriki, Mingei, Tsujuko, and Toyogami from Japan. Fabriano text from Italy and domestic papers that do not fade in the light are best. Scores of beautifully colored tissue papers that fade very rapidly are tempting to use but have almost no permanence. If you evaluate these colored papers as you would oil pigments and apply the same standards of stability, you will avoid the cheap dyed papers that are not designed to last. There are many buffs, off-white, and grey sheets that are color-fast, subtle, and quite suitable for chine collé work.

To complete a print in this process, after your etched plate has been brought to the desired state (it may be aquatint, soft-ground, lift-ground, dry point, and so on), you must decide on the areas to be colored. Design it on tracing paper or thin bond paper. Choose your colored paper and trace or score the shape of the area onto its back surface. Cut or tear the shapes to the proper size. These pieces should be dampened between blotters or newsprint until they are uniformly moist, with no surface water or drops showing. Dampening may take several hours, the time depending on the paper used. Your etching plate may be inked and wiped in the normal manner. Use a few drops of oil of cloves (Eugenol) in the ink to retard the drying process. Now turn all your damp pieces of colored paper, face down, on a clean newsprint, and brush a thin even coat of dilute library paste or thin potato starch over the back of the pieces. The wiped etching plate is placed on the bed of the press, the colored paper is placed face down, (glued side up), in position, on the plate; the printing paper, dampened in the usual manner, is put over all, with adequate margins, and then the plate is printed in the usual manner.

The ink will be printed on top of the pieces of colored paper, and the color will appear underneath your network of lines and tones, glued in position on the backing paper.

Misch Kohn
"Ornate Figure"
Chine collé and lift ground etching 34¼" x 17¾"
Weyhe Gallery

CHINE COLLÉ PROCESS

inked and wiped intaglio plate on press bed

colored paper in position on top of intaglio plate. Glue side up

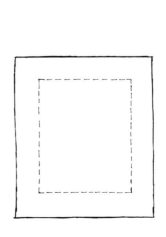

Dampened rag paper over all

The Collagraph

A new printmaking technique, most frequently called the collagraph, has been appearing in exhibitions with great regularity in the last few years. The collagraph, as generally defined, is a print of a collage of a wide variety of materials glued together on masonite, cardboard, or a metal plate. Any fairly rigid material such as lucite or plexiglass can be used. The collagraph differs from the cardboard relief print in that it is printed as an intaglio plate or as a combined intaglio and relief plate. The word *collagraph* should not be confused with the term *collotype*. A collotype is a mechanical printing process developed in the late 19th century that uses a photo gelatin process for reproduction.

Various terms have been used for the medium, such as collage intaglio, collage print, collagraph or collagraphy. We prefer the term *collagraph*, as coined by Glen Alps, because it seems to describe the technique best. The derivation of the word tells much about it. The word *collagraph* stems from the Greek term *colla*, meaning glue, or the French *coller*, to glue, and from the English word *graphic* pertaining

Glen Alps
"Three Chickens" 1958
Collagraph, 22½" x 33½"
Courtesy of the artist
Photograph Whitie Marten

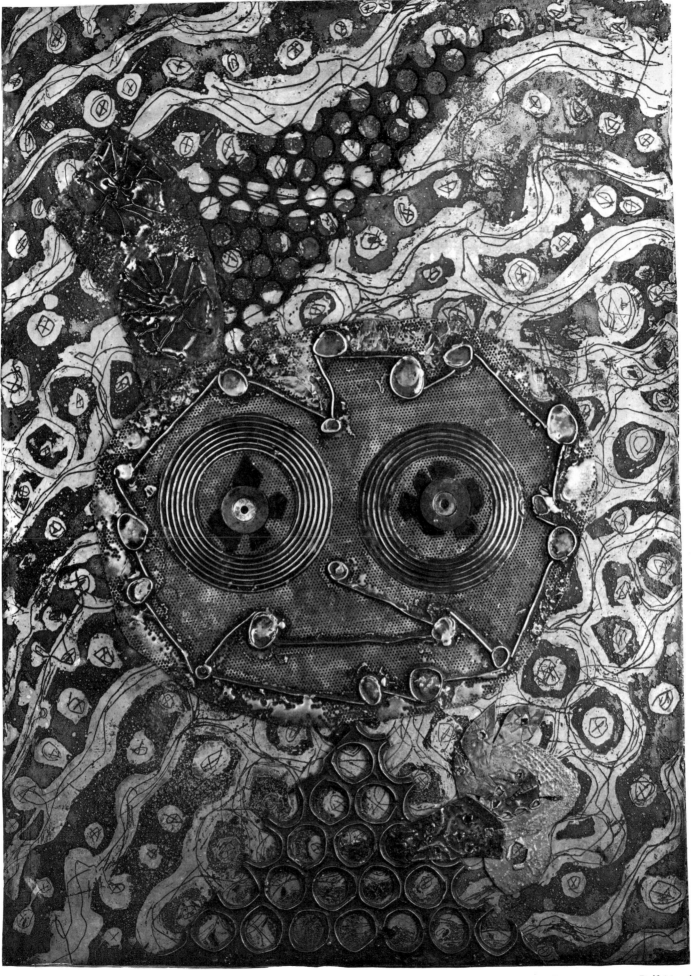

Rolf Nesch
"Toy" 1965 (Plate)
Metal collage plate 22⁹⁄₁₆″ x 16½″
Collection Walter Bareiss

to written or drawn material. The main function of any descriptive word is to clarify a process for the general public. As long as artists remain individualists they will use a variety of terms for similar processes.

The historical evolvement of the collagraph would be difficult to trace. As early as the late 19th century, prints have appeared that indicate that adhesives were applied to copper or zinc plates and then inked and printed.

The innovating experiments with collage and assemblage by the early 20th-century French artists, such as Picasso, Matisse, and Gris, did much to open the way for the later printmaker's use of unorthodox materials. This freedom of concept and use of materials had a direct influence on many contemporary printmakers. Rolf Nesch, the Norwegian printmaker, was one of the first artists to use an assembled plate in the 1930s. His material was primarily metal, and his work is described as a metal collage with some forms soldered in place and other forms cut and assembled unadhered for printing.

The collagraph seems to have evolved directly from the concepts of Nesch, with the addition of more flexible materials. Numerous artists have developed personal methods from this approach. Glen Alps, printmaker and professor at the University of Washington in Seattle, was an early innovator with the collagraph. His experiments with collage intaglio with his students led him to a creative use of the medium. He was the first to use the term *collagraph* as a means to describe the technique. James Steg, a professor at Newcomb College of Tulane University in New Orleans and Dean Meeker, at the University of Wisconsin, have developed personal statements through the collagraph.

Our own development of the collagraph grew out of our use of the cardboard and paper relief print. For a number of years in the 1950s we found the flexibility of cardboard an excellent vehicle for large color prints. We glued various thicknesses and textures of cardboard and paper on either cardboard or Masonite for our images. Sometimes we used a three-ply chip board and cut into it with X-acto knives and razor blades, much as the woodcut is cut. We glued a variety of materials such as textured papers, cloth, lace, metal objects, and sand to the relief plates to develop surface variations. The tonal nuances were interesting and rewarding. Later, as we began to work with etching, we felt the need to use the intaglio in a more flexible manner. When John Ross was artist in residence in 1964 with the United States Information Agency exhibition "Graphic Arts USA" in Romania, he began to experiment with plates made out of cardboard, paper, and cloth and any found objects that would print and relate to the image. The response to the experimental medium by Romanian artists was very enthusiastic, as their use of the print had been most often traditional in concept.

The intaglio plate is developed through the subtractive procedure of acid biting the image into copper or zinc. It

Opposite:
John Ross
"Vertical Forces" 1967
Color collagraph 21½" x 14"

A collagraph, with a sand texture yielding a deep black at top. A hex nut gives its distinctive form to the center area. Other forms are cut cardboad, paper, and sheet metal glued into the plate.

Below: An antique coin was imbedded into a mat board plate and its embossed forms catch the ink and print. Print by Ross.

can be a long, painstaking process. Its scope is tremendous, the range of tonal development unique. The collagraph does not displace the etching image but introduces possibilities for a different kind of statement through the variety of materials available and the ease and flexibility in developing a collage plate.

RELATING IMAGE TO MATERIALS AND TECHNIQUES

The actual assembly and creation of a collage plate is physically simple, but it has its pitfalls. The major cliche to avoid is an overdependence on the material. It is easy to become trapped by the rich quality of surface and texture that comes from the simplest piece of cloth, tarletan, or lace glued down on a firm surface, then inked, wiped, and printed as an intaglio. The same entrapment awaits the artist in his first use of soft-ground etching. The materials impressed in their natural state can begin to dominate the artist instead of being used by him as a vehicle towards expressing a personal statement.

There are numerous helpful suggestions that we can make at this point. If the artist has some experience with etching and knows the tonalities possible through the use of aquatint, soft-ground textures, and wiping, he will feel more secure and will be able to plan and visualize in relation to a past body of experiences. If the artist has done some work with relief methods, in color and black-and-white, through relief etching, woodcut, or collage relief, he will be able to use the medium as a combination of intaglio and relief in a more inventive and personal way.

Materials for the Collagraph

The materials suggested here are easily available to anyone, and the items are inexpensive. These materials we have found particularly useful. You will add other things relating to the needs of your own expression.

Two and three-ply cardboard and chipboard, thin cardboard such as used by laundries in packaging shirts.

⅛″ to ¼″ tempered Masonite, 2-ply cardboard or zinc plates, heavy acetate, or lucite to be used as bases for gluing.

Paper (for cutting images, not printing) in an endless variety of thickness and texture from heavy watercolor paper to thin tissue paper to paper doilies.

Cloth in all textures from fine silk to burlap.

Novelty fabrics, such as lace, rick rack, cloth tapes, or embroidered fabrics.

Wire, metal screening, metal washers, a wide variety of hardware store items that are meaningful to your image.

Found objects, such as gaskets, bottie caps, coins, or old container lids, sometimes with relief lettering. The range is wide open as long as the object is printable.

Sandpaper, from fine to rough, beach and builder's sand, coffee grounds, metal filings, sawdust, even cat litter has been used. Crushed walnut shells have also been used to hold black tones by Glen Alps in some of his prints.

Used photoengraving plates, paper mat plates.

Acrylic gesso and Elmer's glue for gluing, polymer medium, sobo modeling paste, clear plastic spray can.

Razor blades (industrial, single-edge may be purchased cheaply in boxes of 100 in discount drug stores).

Single-edge razor-blade holder, available in most hardware stores.

X-acto knives with interchangeable small blades, excellent for fine work.

Large and small scissors.

Scoring tools such as nail punches, wheels, and rasps.

Brushes of all sizes.

Palette and painting knives.

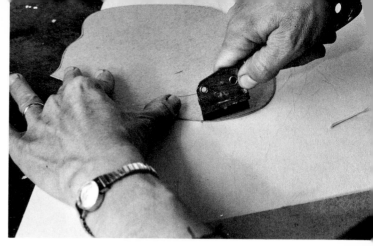

Cutting cardboard for a paper relief plate or a collagraph requires fresh razor blades and a good blade holder.

ASSEMBLING THE PLATE

The actual procedure for assembling a plate is dictated in part by the methods most comfortable for the artist. If he is used to working freely without thinking out the images, he will no doubt feel at home with assembling his materials and immediately cutting and arranging them in a spontaneous way, as he would approach the creation of a collage. Very often it is difficult to predict the actual tonalities of the collage materials before they are printed. However, soft pencil, charcoal, colored pencils, and pastels can indicate directions for the artist to follow. He may feel more secure if a finished sketch to size, tonality, and color is prepared. It is impossible to prescribe the best method. The artist has to determine it through his choice of image.

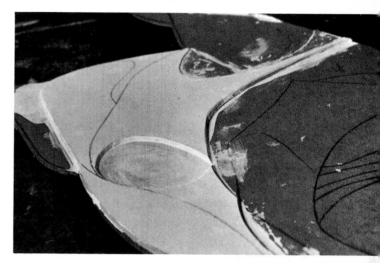

Cut the edges at a bevel to facilitate printing. Polymer acrylic gesso is used as the glue and the sealant.

One way to understand the full potential of the medium is to prepare an experimental plate with a great variety of materials, objects, and methods.

Take a piece of ⅛″ tempered Masonite or cardboard at least 12″ by 15″ and, with either Elmer's glue or gesso, adhere a variety of materials to it. Coat the surface of the plate well with glue where the piece of paper, cardboard, cloth, or object is to be placed, as well as the back of the material. After pressing it into place, be sure it is well secured with no edges or areas lifting. If the material or object is difficult to manage, use weights to hold it down. If cardboard or some similar thick material is being cut into a form to be glued in position, bevel the edges so that it will be easier to print.

When cloths, lace, string, or thin materials such as paper or tissues are used, glue the top surfaces too, in order to lock them in position more securely.

Larger pieces may have to be weighted during the gluing process. The edges should be firmly glued and sealed.

Other materials, fabrics, paper, buttons, coins, and such may be glued to the base board.

Below: Both sides should be glued. The gesso is very resilient and will not crack, even under pressure. It is waterproof when dry.

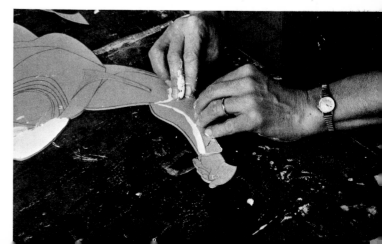

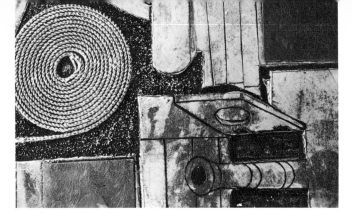

Twine, sandpaper, coarse sand, cardboard, and bitten zinc plate etchings are included in this section of a plate.

An old coin, cut paper, and an aquatint etching make up this part of a collagraph.

If particles such as sand, coffee grounds, sawdust, or crushed walnut shells are being used, coat the surface of the plate well with Elmer's glue or gesso and sprinkle the material into the wet adhesive. After it is dry, apply a coat of gesso or glue to the surface.

Cut into the cardboard, Masonite, or acetate, or lucite plate to see the potential of incised lines.

If many varying textured materials are used, you will learn how they wipe and produce a variety of tonalities when printed. Cloth that varies from fine silk to burlap will produce different tonalities. Papers such as watercolor or charcoal or etching paper will give similar results. Oilcloth will wipe very clean, giving an almost white quality. Smooth papers will give very light tonalities. Sandpaper, sand, sawdust, coffee grounds, carborundum, cat litter, or crushed walnut shells will all hold a large amount of ink and print quite black.

If the cardboard or Masonite is not large enough for all these materials, make more than one experimental plate.

Another plate could contain pure gesso, Elmer's glue, polymer, or any similar material. These materials can be used like paint with both stiff and soft-bristled brushes to give variety to the line or mass. Allow the material to dry well and then spray it with a liquid plastic to make wiping easier. Allow the plate to dry very well before printing.

If Masonite is used as a base, be sure to bevel the sides of the plate well with a file just as a metal plate is beveled, to ease printing and to avoid sharp plate marks in the blankets.

In an ordinary etching press such as the Brand press, it is wise not to build the plate up higher than two to three thicknesses of matboard or the height of Masonite and one cardboard without special matrixes and devices or the use

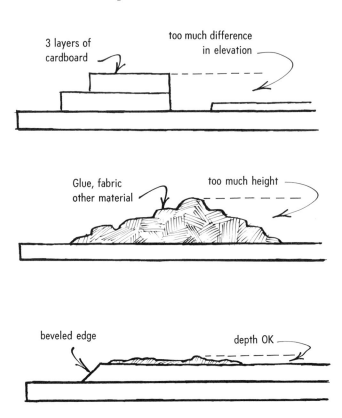

COLLAGRAPH THICKNESS

Acrylic polymer gesso was sponged on top of a lightly aquatinted tone. The deep black lines have been bitten through soft ground. Print by Ross.

of a direct drive press. It is unwise to try to run thick objects or single raised objects of more than these heights through the press.

INKING THE COLLAGRAPH

Before any inking is done, be very sure all the materials are adhered very well to the plate. You may spray it with a clear plastic spray to facilitate wiping. The inking process is essentially the same as used in inking an etching plate. Any previous experience in etching is extremely useful.

We have found small 2″ by 3″ or 2½″ by 2½″ squares of matboard very useful in inking a collagraph plate. They are easily made and can be used and discarded at will. The sharp corners are very good for forcing the ink into small areas and corners. The flat edge can pull and push the ink and also force it into textured areas. This method is very good for plates with large raised areas and textured areas.

Felt daubers are often used by etchers for inking. However, the daubers get very stiff from dry ink, and perpetual trimming of the end is necessary to keep it supple. Sometimes a stiff stipple brush is very good for a low-relief, very textured plate. Our students have used toothbrushes and nailbrushes for inking.

We find black Cronite ink very adequate for the collagraph because it is a fairly soft ink and easily wiped. Graphic Chemical makes a superior ink that is fairly stiff. With a mixing knife, mix about a teaspoon of plate oil with an area of ink about 6″ in diameter on a slab. Both Cronite and Graphic Chemical ink often require the addition of plate oil to insure easy wiping. A few drops of oil of cloves is a necessary addition to the ink to retard drying when inking becomes a lengthy process.

Put a generous amount of ink all over the plate. Spread the ink with the cardboards until every tiny area is covered. Use fresh cardboards whenever they become soft. Scrape all the excess ink off the plate and put it back into the can. Continue until only a moderate amount of ink is left on the plate.

Have two pieces of tarletan about 15″ by 30″ ready for wiping. One tarletan with a deposit of ink already on it should function as the dirty tarletan, and the other should be fairly clean, for clean wiping.

Many etchers have rather rigid rules about how the tarletan should be used. We prefer to leave procedures flexible. Arrange the dirty tarletan in a rather loose ball with a flat side for wiping. The dirty tarletan provides a preliminary clean-up for the plate. Press it into small areas and deep textures to remove excess ink. Use its flat side for broad areas until much of the excess ink is removed. Now use the clean tarletan to wipe the surface well until the textures on the plate are easily seen. Some hand wiping is now desirable to bring out structures on the plate. Wipe with the fleshy underpart of the palm, using broad strokes. Wipe the palm frequently with a clean cloth to make the wiping effective. If very light tones are desired in some areas, or on raised surfaces, use a small piece of newsprint paper, ordinary newspaper, or paper toweling held flat to gently wipe over the surfaces to produce a lighter quality. Change the paper frequently to insure clean wiping.

The basic inking starts with the thick plate ink applied all over the plate with small squares of cut matboard.

Paper wiping helps to polish the areas that must be especially well cleaned.

In deep recesses a stiff stencil brush helps to spread the viscous plate ink.

The raised areas of the collagraph plate are rolled with brayers inked with an ink of less viscosity than the plate ink used for the base color.

The plate ink is wiped with a pad of tarletan or crinoline. This process removes most of the ink from the surface areas. Gloves help to keep hands clean.

Clare Romano prepares a segmented collagraph plate by placing the inked pieces of thin cardboard into position.

The hand wipe brings up the rich textural detail. Light, fast strokes with the edge of the palm work well.

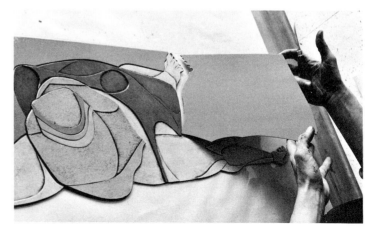

The final piece of the cut plate is put in place; sometimes tweezers or pins are necessary to keep the freshly inked segments from smearing.

PAPER DAMPENING

For proving, an inexpensive paper like index or basing-werk is adequate. Soak the paper from 5 to 15 minutes, depending on its weight. A lighter paper will need less time. A tray of water to soak the paper is necessary. After soaking, hold the paper over the water tray with 2"-square paper or metal grippers to keep the paper clean. An artist we know uses plastic-coated wallet-size calendars that are printer's rejects for this purpose. They work beautifully because they repell water. Thin metal strips can also be used. Allow all the excess water to drip back into the tray. When occasional drops drain off, the paper is easier to blot and will not be too wet for printing. Roll the top blotter with a large hard rubber roller or a rolling pin to help the blotters absorb the water. Murillo, a buff paper of fairly heavy quality made by Fabriano of Italy, is excellent. Italia and Rives BFK and German Etching are white papers that produce fine results. All these papers are excellent for edition work. The choice of weight and color and texture of the paper to be used will be determined by the depth of the plate, color used.

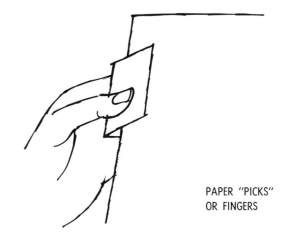

PAPER "PICKS"
OR FINGERS

PRINTING

Procedures in printing a collagraph are very varied. So much depends on the height of the plate and the materials used. When the collagraph is printed in one color in an ordinary etching press, certain controls should be observed so that the bed and the roller are not damaged. The plate should generally not have more than ⅛" variation in height from the top of the printing surface to the lower printing surface.

Set the press for the desired pressure, which must be determined by experimentation. Place a sheet of clean newsprint on the press bed to keep it clean. Place the inked plate on the newsprint paper. Place a 1" sheet of foam rubber over the plate to absorb impressions from raised objects. Use another blanket over the foam rubber. An inexpensive dark grey, unwoven wool about ¼" thick is a good second blanket. Smooth the blankets to be sure they are sitting well on the plate and begin to engage the roller over the plate. You will be able to get the feel of the proper pressure by the ease with which the roller travels over the plate. If it is too tight, reduce the pressure. If it feels too loose, tighten it. After rolling it through at the proper pressure, pull the paper off the plate slowly to be sure no areas are adhering to the plate. If excess ink appears on the proof, blot it with a clean piece of newsprint by rubbing your palm over the surface of the newsprint paper. Examine the print to see how to proceed. Write down the pressure used for printing, and the blankets used. Keep an accurate note so that all the same conditions may be attained in the next proving.

Excess moisture is removed by placing the paper between two clean blotters and pressing the sheets together with a rolling pin.

Drying Print

The easiest way to insure a collagraph's drying flat is to staple it to a homosote board or wall and allow it to stretch flat as it dries. Place staples 1½" apart to insure even drying. However, as stretching inevitably means the loss of a great deal of the depth of the embossing, you may allow the print to dry on a flat blotter for one half to one hour depending on the room temperature. Then pin or staple it to a wall in a semi-dry state. In this way much of the embossing is retained. A more dependable way to hold all the depth in the embossing is to dry the prints flat between clean white flat blotters, about one inch larger than the print. Lay them on a clean large flat surface, and place about two blotters between successive prints. Place a medium weight, the size of the blotters on top of the pile. A piece of masonite or plywood is a good choice. Allow the prints to dry overnight. Replace the blotters with dry clean blotters and repeat again overnight. After 48 hours the prints should be dry and the paper flat with all the embossing just as it was printed.

Another excellent way to dry prints flat is to stack the prints between blotters placed between sheets of ⅛" asbestos board. Warrington Colescott finds this method very efficient because the asbestos does not absorb moisture. However, care should be taken not to breathe the dust when cutting asbestos because it is very harmful.

Clean Up

By the time you are working with the collagraph you should have had some experience with woodcut and etching. The clean-up is the same. The plate must be cleaned thoroughly of all the ink and wiped dry. Slabs, mixing knives, and inking counter should be left clean and neat for next day's printing.

PRINTING PROBLEMS AND REMEDIES

Problem: Ink runs on print, large deposits of ink around forms.

Remedy: Pressure is too great, and too much ink has been left in lines or between forms. Ink may also contain too much oil. Reduce pressure, wipe cleaner, add more pigment to ink, and reduce amount of plate oil.

Problem: Paper sticking to plate or tearing.

Remedy: Pressure may be too great, also ink may be too stiff; add plate oil. Ink may be drying on plate because of long inking time; add a few drops of oil of cloves in addition to plate oil; reduce inking time. Carefully and slowly remove print from plate to avoid tearing, avoid over-dampening paper.

Problem: Uneven printing because of varying heights.

Remedy: If there are different levels on the plate and some areas are not printing well, foam-rubber blankets can be cut to fit into low areas to improve overall pressure. Sometimes dampened blotters placed between the printing paper and foam rubber blankets help to achieve uniform printing.

Problem: Wrinkles in paper as plate is printed.

Remedy: Blankets may be too stiff from deposits of sizing. Paper may be too wet or unevenly dampened, or paper may be of improper weight, probably too thin. Wash blankets often in detergent solution for wool to keep them soft. Try other papers.

Problem: White areas around forms, uneven inking.

Remedy: Pressure may be too little, increase pressure;

Stanley William Hayter
"Danae"
Color Intaglio 22¹⁵⁄₁₆″ x 16⅝″
Collection Manhattanville College

plate may not be inked enough; blankets may need washing; forms may not be beveled enough for paper to make contact.

MULTICOLOR COLLAGRAPH

The flexibility of the collagraph lends itself to a very expansive use of color. Its potential for multicolor work on one plate is excellent. Because the method is an additive one, the necessary variety of levels for printing can be more easily achieved than with acid biting into metal. The creative use of one plate in multicolor printing has been extensively explored by William Hayter and many of the artists who worked closly with him in Atelier 17 in Paris in the thirties, New York City in the forties, and back in Paris in the fifties and sixties. Hayter's book, "New Ways of Gravure," is useful for artists who wish to deal extensively with one-plate color printing. Hayter's methods utilize the deeply bitten plate as a way to use color on different levels. His experiments with inks of varying viscosities and rollers of different hardness and softness are among the most important aspects of his technique. See our description of the Hayter method of multicolor printing in the intaglio section.

We will attempt to explain some of our methods and the methods of other artists using color in the collagraph so that the artist using color in one-plate printing can have as many resources as possible at his disposal.

Inking of Plate as Combined Intaglio and Relief

Any intaglio plate has the potential of being inked as a combination intaglio and relief plate. Even a simple line-bite etching with moderate bite can be inked in the recessions with one color, with a second color rolled on the surface with a gelatin, plastic, or hard-rubber roller, depending on the nature of the image. Without much difficulty a two-color etching is achieved.

The first color or base color, inked in the intaglio method, can be applied in the same manner described under "Inking the Plate" in the intaglio section. The choice of color for the base color is limited only by the etching colors on hand. Some colors need the application of plate oil to make wiping easier. The addition of a few drops of oil of cloves to the color will keep it from drying, and we use it for both the base colors and the relief colors. The wiping will depend on the color and the image. Because the etching ink is of heavy viscosity it will remain in the recessions. After the base color is wiped, a soft plastic roller can be used to add another color of medium viscosity such as letterpress ink to some surface areas as well as to recessions. The lower viscosity of this ink prevents it from pulling up the intaglio ink. Where still other colors are desired for other relief areas, small rollers can be used to add color or the relief areas can be wiped clean and color added with small rollers to produce the greater clarity of a single color. A hard roller with ink of even lesser viscosity will allow deposits of ink on high relief and not in recessions. In order to make the ink less viscous or sticky, add a little plate oil to the ink until the desired consistency is found. The more small rollers you have on hand to provide variation in hardness and softness, from gelatin to soft plastic to hard rubber, the more flexibility there will be in the use of color. Sometimes the rollers can be used to remove color from certain areas in a plate so that a color applied to the clean area can sing out clearly and brilliantly.

In some complicated color procedures a stencil of commercial frisket paper or acetate sheets can be used to mask out certain areas on a plate to ease inking. One student used a stencil very successfully to ink only certain areas in a complicated plate that was to be inkless embossing except for a few areas.

Printing the Color Collagraph

The length of time required for inking depends on the complexity of the plate. The less time it takes to ink the plate the better. If a plate takes more than one hour there is a danger that the ink will dry and not print in dry areas. Place the plate on a large sheet of acetate to protect the press bed. Guide marks for placing the plate can be scored in the acetate or marked on a piece of newsprint paper under the acetate. Guides for paper can be designated on the press bed with masking tape. Acetate is useful because it can be easily wiped clean of ink. Take the paper out of the water, blot it, and so on, as described earlier in the intaglio section, and place it on the plate. Place a piece of newsprint paper over the etching paper to absorb moisture and to keep the blankets dry. Add necessary blankets, adjust pressure, and roll the plate through.

If there are metal objects incorporated in the plate, it is wise to use a piece of 1½″ or 2″ foam rubber next to the plate and then one of the dark grey blankets over the foam rubber. This padding will protect the more expensive white woven felt blankets and keep them in reserve for printing more evenly surfaced collagraphs or etchings.

After the plate has been fully developed and proved, and an edition is desired, we have found the preparation of a *printing procedure diagram* of invaluable assistance for

Clare Romano
"Zagreb Night" 1966
Color collagraph 22″ x 26¼″
 and etching

future printing. Like many other contemporary printmakers, we do not print our editions immediately after completing a plate. We often will print 10 or 12 of an edition and then go on to new work. We return to finishing the edition when printing time is more available or the demand for a given print requires printing. To construct a printing procedure diagram, we pull a newsprint impression of every plate after the finished print has been pulled. The residue remaining on the plate is sufficient to give us the basic structure of the image with a good indication of color areas for future reference. We then key areas of the print to the rollers used, write out color mixing recipes for difficult colors to mix, general wiping procedures, press pressure, number of blankets used, type and order of placement on the plate, and paper used. All our rollers are numbered for easy keying because rollers of different softness and hardness are needed for the various surfaces. Our total roller count runs close to 90 at this writing. Relief color can be saved for re-use or easier mixing by tightly wrapping it in wax paper packets, and intaglio color in large quantities can be stored in cans. If these procedures are kept uniform, the general printing quality of an edition is easily sustained even with long periods of time between printings.

Cut Plate Printing

In some color printing the best and most versatile solution for the use of many colors, especially if great clarity and brilliance is desired, is to cut the plate apart. With cardboard or Masonite plates, this is very easy and with metal plates a power jigsaw produces very good results. The plates can be cut very precisely, inked separately, then reassembled for printing on the bed of the press and run through in one operation.

Collagraph and Etching Combination

At various times we have combined the traditionally bitten, engraved, or drypoint metal plates with the collagraph plates. We have used etching-gauge zinc and copper and sheet copper and lithograph zinc depending upon the purpose.

Our combination of methods has met our need to combine a delicacy of line and tone with the freedom of the collagraph. The metal plates can be glued into the collage with gesso or other strong adhesives or printed separately as an assembled plate. Particular care must be given to inking a plate with such a combination because the wiping needs of each plate differ.

Photoengraving cuts may also be combined successfully into a plate. We have achieved the best results when the cuts were assembled into the plate without gluing. The cuts print more clearly when rolled as relief plates with hard rollers and thin applications of relief ink.

Photoengraving cuts discarded by photoengraving companies can sometimes be an interesting addition to an image if there is a conceptual reason for their inclusion. Like many mechanical devices they can be overused and become very cliché if not thoughtfully incorporated in an image. They often appear as part of the assemblage of materials in the prints of Clare Romano.

A half-tone relief plate has been inked with a brayer and placed into an intgalio wiped collagraph by Clare Romano.

PHOTOGRAPHIC TECHNIQUES

INTRODUCTION

The images that photography can capture have caused many artists to develop techniques designed to exploit the photographic process. These techniques are suitable for many areas of printmaking, such as lithography on metal plates, etching on zinc or copper, photo-silk screen and relief etching on metal plates. There are many approaches to photography in printmaking, and they vary from straightforward reproduction of photographs, such as Andy Warhol's screen prints *Jackie* and *Marilyn*, through Robert Rauschenberg's more complex lithographs to Joe Tilson's and Eduardo Paolozzi's prints combining screen printing and lithography.

It is possible to use images on photoengraving plates made by a commercial engraver by relief rolling the image with a good quality brayer and then transferring that image to an etching or a litho plate. The photoengraving can also be printed directly into your print. Negative effects will be produced by intaglio inking and wiping followed by printing the plate through an etching press. Plastic mats, electrotypes, and commercially prepared litho plates can be incorporated into the print, either directly or by the transfer method. Collage plates can accomodate a variety of photographically produced images (See Lindner's *The Parrot Lady*).

However, if an artist wants to make his own photographic plates he can use a number of different methods to place the image onto the plate or stencil. We will describe several processes and note the advantages and disadvantages of each.

THE TRANSPARENT POSITIVE

(Acetate, Paper, Glass, and the Like)

In many cases it will be advisable to have your image put on transparent film (usually Mylar or Estar based for dimensional stability). Other transparent sheets can be used, however, with good results. For instance, you can draw with any opaque ink or pencil on a thin, good-quality tracing paper to make a transparent positive through which light can pass

A half-tone plate, from a commercial photo engravers shop, is inked with a 6-inch plastic composition roller. A thin even film of ink is necessary.

Below: The impression from the half-tone engraving is transferred to the stone from an 8-inch plastic roller.

65

A zinc plate lithograph may be printed in an etching press with excellent results. A student of Jack Sonenberg at Pratt Institute in Brooklyn is about to place the dampened paper on the plate.

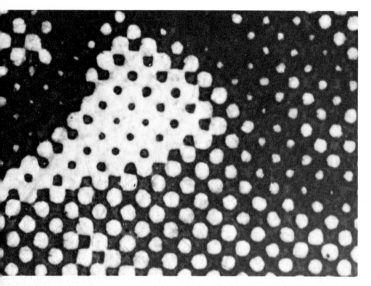

The half-tone dot breaks up the picture into thousands of black or white dots of varying size, depending on the depth of tonality in the original copy.

to expose the sensitized plate or stencil. You can also use cellophane or acetate as a base and paint or draw on it with non-crawl paint, ink, or crayon. There is a prepared acetate sheet that will accept water-based paint without bubbling or shrinking. You can even paint or draw on glass to make a transparent positive.

In general, two types of positives are used in photographic work. A line shot is one in which all the image is translated into black or white lines or masses. The film used is not sensitive to greys and renders them as either black or white, depending upon their density. Solid areas are flat. Greys must be achieved by texture or a network of fine lines.

The second photographic process, called half-tone, renders grey values by breaking up the areas into black and white dots of varying sizes. A finely ruled screen is placed between the art work and the film, separating the picture into thousands of tiny squares, each one registering as a single dot, of a size commensurate with its grey value. The screens range in fineness from a low of 40 or 45 to a normal high of 133 lines to the inch. Some screens go up to 300 lines, but they are too fine for normal commercial printing. Screens are quite expensive and must be handled with care, as one scratch can ruin the ruled surface. The coarser screens are easier to print. A delicate wash drawing or a subtle grey photographic tone will reproduce in correct values, by virtue of the tiny dots of black. These half-tone dots can be seen in an enlarging glass.

Positive Transparencies with the Copy Camera

Although a copy camera setup is not inexpensive (a good 14" by 17" camera costs about $2000), it is the most efficient instrument for producing consistently good transparencies to be used in photographic printmaking. These films can be used in many ways and in many processes, such as screen printing, lithography, intaglio etching, and relief etching. A trained technician is desirable to help the artist achieve the best results from his material.

The step-by-step procedure of making transparencies will be described, using commonly available materials, such as Kodalith Ortho #3 film, no. 4556, which can be used for both line and half-tone shots (Gevaert 082 Film can also be used). Exposures range from 20 seconds to 1 minute, depending on the intensity of the lights and the density of the material to be photographed. The half-tone shot needs a longer exposure than the line shot. This film is sensitive to yellow light and needs a red safelight in the darkroom. The photographs show the procedures. When the first film has been developed, washed, and dried, you will have a negative transparency, with the originally black lines now showing as white on a black background.

To make a positive transparency, place the negative back on the camera in the horizontal position, on top of another piece of Kodalith Ortho #3, 4556. Place a piece of clear glass on top of both, if necessary, to assure good contact. Expose for 30 seconds in yellow light. Develop, stop, fix, and wash as described above. This exposure will make the positive transparency, with the lines that were black in the original now black in the transparency. This exposure can be made in a

The copy to be photographed is placed in the copy board vacuum frame. (Line drawing by Al Blaustein.)

The copy board is sealed and the vacuum pump operated to insure that the drawing has good contact with the glass.

The copy is placed in a vertical position by Donna Moran, technician at Pratt Institute in Brooklyn.

Exposure and focus are computed and the camera is adjusted. The lens opening is set.

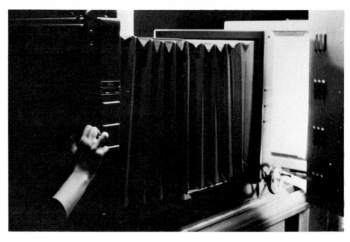

Both ends of the bellows may be adjusted. Focus can be checked on the ground glass at the back of camera.

Two vertical rows of lights are positioned to properly illuminate the copy.

Below: The film holder (back) of the camera is lowered. When film is inserted, only a red safelight may be used. The light at the top of this photo is a yellow light and is used for a "bump" exposure on half-tones to extend the grey scale. For this procedure the back is opened flat. This step completes the exposure.

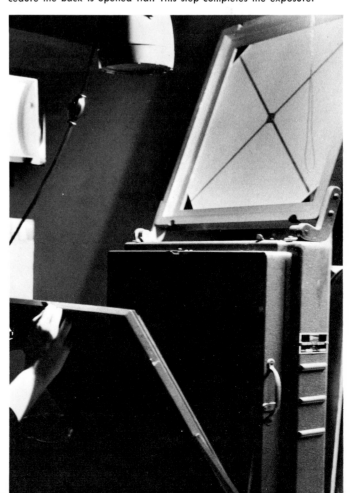

Still in red safelight, the film is inserted into the developer. Kodalith liquid developer, 1 part A solution, 1 part B solution, 6 cups of water at 70°, for 2½ minutes average time.

From developer to stop bath (4 ounces of acetic acid to a gallon of water). Then into 3M Rapid Fix or Kodak Liquid Fix Concentrate with hardener for three times the length of time it takes to clear. Then wash in water at 70° for 10 minutes.

Below: Hang film to dry after it has been squeegeed to remove excess water. This process has produced a negative transparency.

vacuum frame, if available, or on a table top with any available high-intensity light. You will now have, on transparent film, a photographic image that can be used in a variety of media.

Positive Transparencies with an Enlarger

Small photographic negatives can be enlarged onto Kodalith Ortho #3 film, up to the greatest size the enlarger can handle. A certain amount of detail is always lost in excessive blow-ups, and a sharp edge is difficult to achieve. The enlarger should have a condenser system to concentrate the light rather than diffuse it, and the lens should be a high-resolution lens that can produce good definition. 35 mm. or 2¼"-square negatives will lose sharpness when enlarged 10 times or more. The Kodalith film will translate certain types of negatives that do not rely upon tonal gradations without a halftone screen, with occasionally unusual effects. Of course, if you use a normal negative your enlarged transparency on Kodalith will be a positive and will yield a positive intaglio plate or, conversely, a negative-relief etching plate. Film negatives exposed onto an etching plate will yield a negative intaglio or a positive relief etching plate.

PHOTO-ETCHING

In general there are two approaches to photo-etching a zinc or copper plate to prepare it for intaglio or relief printing. The first method involves sensitizing the plate yourself with a solution that will react to light. The second method involves buying a presensitized plate from a commercial photoengravers supply house. Both methods are suitable, depending on your location and the quantity of plates which you consume. The commercially prepared plates have a uniform coating that gives high-quality results. They must be stored carefully, in a cool place, and should be used within a few months. The additional cost per plate is moderate (about $1 extra per plate). The self-prepared plates can be made as you choose, and the chemicals have a shelf life of about a year. Unless you prepare the plate properly you may not get results as good as from a commercially sensitized plate. We will describe both processes.

Self-Sensitized Zinc or Copper Plates

The materials needed to sensitize zinc or copper plates include Kodak KPR chemicals, which cost approximately $25:

> 1 qt. KPR Photo Resist
> 1 gal. KPR Photo Resist Developer
> 1 qt. KPR Photo Resist Dye

Also needed are:

> Zinc, copper, or brass plates
> Stainless steel trays
> Acetone
> Webril-wipe or lint-free cloth

The plate should be thoroughly cleaned with acetone and rinsed well with water. Avoid touching the surface. A clean

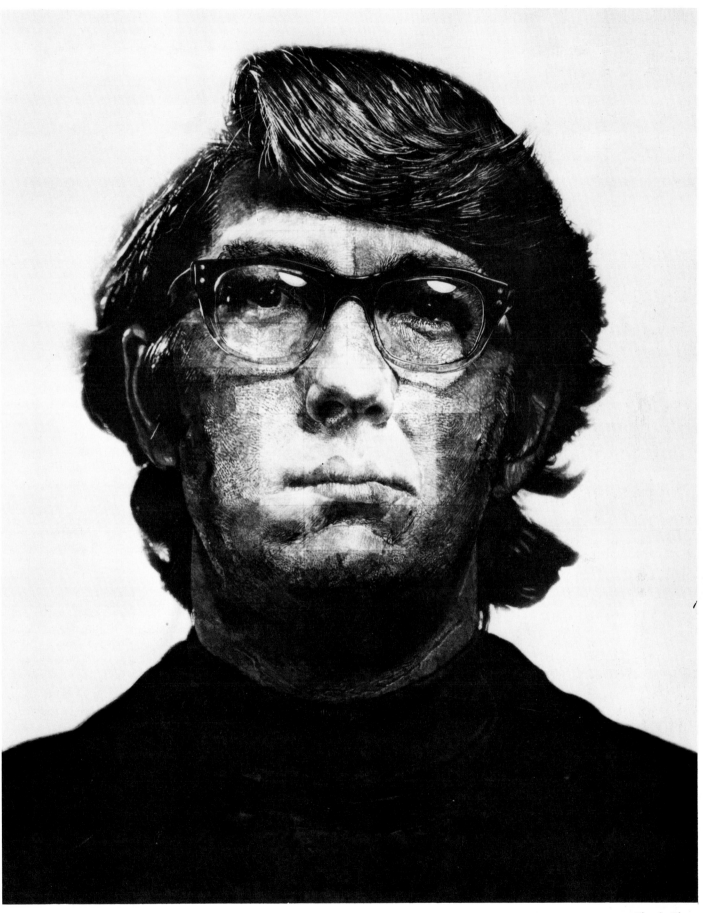

Chuck Close
"Keith"
Intaglio 44½" x 35"
Courtesy Parasol Press
The entire plate was covered with an evenly
etched tone which was then scraped and
burnished to varying tones of grey and
white. Photograph by Nathan Rabin.

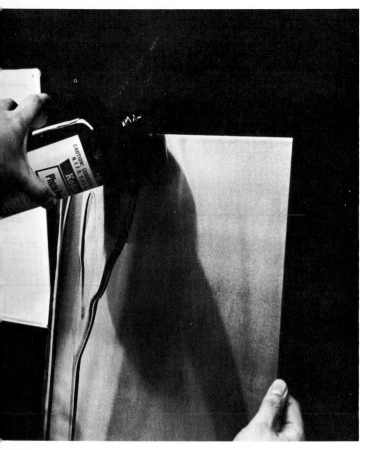

In a darkened room pour the photo-resist fluid over the plate so that it is covered with a thin, even coat.

Below: The plate should be standing in a tray to catch the excess solution for reuse. Let the plate dry.

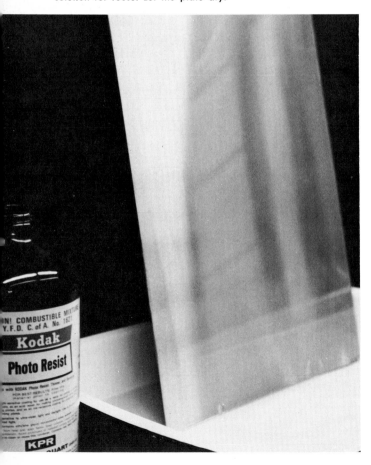

surface is essential, and all grease or dust must be removed. Dry by heat, over hotplate or in oven.

In the darkroom, under a yellow safe light, place the clean plate in a clean tray in a vertical position and pour the Photo Resist over it. The liquid should cover the plate evenly and drain into the tray. The plate can be removed from the tray and leaned against a wall while the remainder of the resist can be funneled back into the bottle. The plate will dry in about 10 to 15 minutes.

Still under the safe light, in the darkroom, place the plate face up on the exposure table, with the film transparency on top. (See section on preparation of transparencies). Cover it with clean glass, either in sheet form or in a vacuum table. The emulsion side of the film should touch the emulsion side of the plate for sharpest results. With a carbon arc lamp, exposure will range from 2 to 4 minutes. With a group of four #1 photoflood lamps in reflectors, exposure could be as long as 20 minutes, but normally it will take somewhat less time.

Remove the plate from the exposing table and slide it into the tray with KPR Photo Resist developer. Develop for 2 or 3 minutes without agitation, then wash the plate with cold water. Pour a coat of KPR Photo Resist dye over the plate while it is in a vertical position, and let it drain for 30 seconds, or submerge the plate in a tray. Place the plate under running water and wash it until the image is visible. The developer can be rebottled and stored in the darkroom.

Now the plate can be etched. Use a weak etching solution (12:1), of nitric acid for zinc or copper and of Dutch Mordant for copper or brass. Ferric chloride is good for very fine biting of copper but must act with the plate face-down in the acid. See section on biting.

To remove the resist prior to printing, wash the plate with lacquer thinner. Bevel the edges and pull the first proofs. Half-tone plates require delicate wiping, and coarse screens work better than fine screens.

Presensitized Zinc or Copper Plates

You may want to use presensitized plates from a local photoengraver's supply house. We use H. Pitman and Sons in Secaucus, New Jersey. These materials may also be obtained from Ball Metal and Chemical Co. in Brooklyn, New York. We use Micro-Metal presensitized plates and the developing solution is, naturally enough, Presensitized Micro-Metal Hi-Speed Developer. Also needed is Presensitized Micro-Metal Print Cleaner Solution. Webril Wipes are convenient to apply the solution. A hotplate is necessary as is some mineral spirits or varnoline.

In the darkroom (yellow safe light) place the presensitized plate on the exposure table face up. Put the film transparency on top of the plate, emulsion side down. Cover with glass or close the vacuum table. If you use an arc lamp, the exposure should be about 3 minutes. Photoflood exposure will take much longer. The light will harden the emulsion where it strikes it. The rest of the emulsion will be softened and washed away by the developer, leaving these areas open to the attack of the acid.

When the exposure is finished place the plate into the developer, either in a tray or in a vertical stainless steel tank.

Place the plate, face up, on the exposure table. Put your photo positive with the desired image on top of the plate. In this case a vacuum frame holds all the elements together, but a piece of plate glass could be sufficient, if handled carefully.

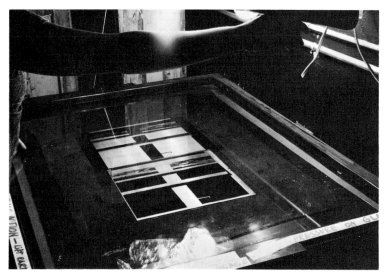

Expose the plate. Normally several minutes are required with photoflood lamps. Carbon arc lamps require only a fraction of the time but are expensive.

Develop the photosensitive emulsion on the plate by immersing it in the developer. Stainless steel trays are best. Some plastics are softened by the photo-resist developer.

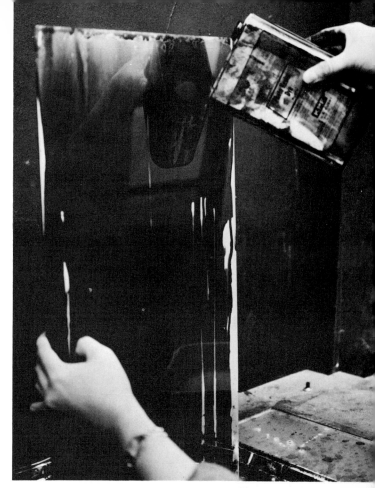

Now stand the plate in another tray and pour photo-resist dye over it so that an even coat drains over the surface. This will stain the developed resist so that the image will be visible.

Wash the plate under running water. The exposed sections will have hardened upon exposure to light and will be insoluble in water.

Below: Bite the plate. It may be aquatinted or retouched first, if desired. (Herb Youner at Pratt Graphic Art Center.)

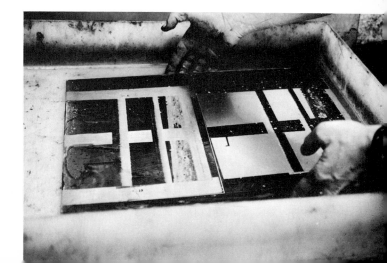

Dennis Rowan
"Femme et Poire" 1969
Etching and Photo
Engraving 36" x 24"
Courtesy of the artist

The sensitivity of this emulsion is not great, and it can be exposed to dim light for brief periods. Remove the plate from the developer and let the excess liquid drain back into the tank. It will stain your hands. Rinse thoroughly with a spray of warm water. Dry with Webril Wipes or a lint free cloth. The image will be visible. Place the plate face up on a table and spread the print cleaner solution over the plate evenly with Webril Wipes. Make sure the plate is completely covered. Rinse again with lukewarm water and then put the plate on the heated hotplate (max. 350°F.) until the water steams off and the blue image changes to a darker brownish color. The topping or resist is now a very hard baked lacquer compound. The plate can be bitten in weak solutions of nitric acid (12:1) or of Dutch Mordant. A 15 to 20 minute bite in 12:1 nitric should be sufficient to etch a half-tone plate. The depth of biting can vary greatly according to the individual plate. One of the great advantages of this method is the ability of the plate to be rebitten, even after it has been inked, wiped, proved, and cleaned. The lacquer topping will withstand all the solvents normally used in the proving process and will enable you to deepen all or part of the plate if you desire. It may be removed with G.A.F. Metal Pyrolidone, if necessary.

The most recent etchings of Peter Milton have been accomplished using a photosensitive ground made by Kodak. A letter from him contains exact, step-by-step procedures for achieving these haunting images:

"This method is essentially parallel to the lift-ground method, but it makes use of more recently developed and considerably more sophisticated materials. It appeals to me because it requires no special equipment beyond a sun-tan bulb and a sheet of plate glass.

"I make my drawing on a sheet of Mylar (or acetate) with a pen and sugar-ink. The sugar-ink has the desired opacity and can be easily removed by gently flaking it off or by rubbing it with a damp tissue. I use the same pen-points as with the lift-ground. In addition, I often begin an image by building up a uniform stipple texture of extremely fine dots, and then forming the image by flaking off dots for the lights and adding dots with a pen for the darks. This is all done by hand and makes no use of photo-engraving aids.

"After the drawing is completed, I coat a copper plate with a photosensitive ground (Kodak KPR 3) which, when dry, is sensitive to ultraviolet light. The coating procedure I use is the simplest: a mixture of equal parts of KPR 3 and KOR thinner is flowed over the plate, which has been elaborately cleaned and prepared. The mixture is allowed to dry with the plate in an upright position. The ground can also be spun on undiluted with a turntable, but I have had no luck with this.

"When the plate has been thoroughly dried of all residual solvents I expose the Mylar drawing onto the plate, using a piece of plate glass for contact pressure and a simple 275 Watt sun-tan bulb for a light source. A typical exposure is 25 minutes at 4½ feet. While a vacuum frame for contact pressure and an arc lamp for exposure would be more professional, I have had perfectly satisfactory results with the simpler and much more easily stored devices.

"The plate is developed in KPR developer. This dissolves the photo-resist wherever there was an opaque mark, but

An exposed presensitized zinc plate is removed from the developing tank at Pratt Institute by Jack Sonenberg. Notice the hooked metal strip used as a holder.

Water at high pressure is sprayed over the developed zinc plate to remove all traces of the developer. Pratt Institute.

doesn't affect any part of the ground which received adequate exposure. The dissolved residue and developer are sprayed off with a gentle aerated spray and the image dyed with KPR dye for better visibility.

"The plate can be etched in the manner normal to any etching procedure. I have obtained best results with 42° Be ferric chloride heated to 100°F., suspending and agitating the plate upside down with the aid of tape handles on the back for small plates and C clamps at the edge for large plates. I use about 5 stopping-out steps and a total final etching time of around 24 minutes.

"The prime advantage of the photosensitive ground procedure is its enormous, almost hair-raising flexibility. Not only can a drawing be transferred at any or all stages of its development, but in any combinations with other drawings, or even high-contrast photographic positive transparencies, all this either simultaneously or at different etching stages— and I have only begun to explore the possibilities.

"This has been a fairly casual explanation about a very exacting set of procedures, and anyone interested can find all the necessary details in the two Kodak pamphlets P-79 and P-125 ($1.00 each, Department 454, Eastman Kodak Co., Rochester, N.Y. 14650)."

Pravoslav Sovak
"With a Tank, August 21, 1968"
Photo Intaglio 16¾" x 12¾"
Pratt Graphics Center
Photo Eric Pollitzer

Opposite:
Peter Milton
from "The Jolly Corner" 1971
Etching and photo-etching 14¾" x 10"
Aquarius Press, Baltimore

Sergio Gonzales-Tornero
"Departure for Venus"
Color Intaglio 23¾" diameter
Courtesy of the artist

CARE
OF PRINTS

MOUNTING PRINTS

Because prints are generally printed on paper, a relatively fragile substance, special care is necessary to preserve them. If a print is going to be sent to an exhibition or even displayed in your studio, a proper mat is an important part of its presentation.

The preparation of the mat is twofold because a mat actually consists of the backing board and the mat. The mat can be hinged to the backing with gummed paper tape for temporary mounting and with gummed linen tape for permanent mounting. A temporary mounting might be used if you are sending out a number of prints to many exhibitions and do not wish to incur great expense. You can use either smooth white matboard or white pebble matboard.

Most exhibitions require clean white mats for uniformity of color and good display technique. Students are sometimes carried away by the wide choice in colored matboard. Try to restrain yourself from being lured by this variety because color generally does not enhance the work.

Matting Material

The backing can be single-weight chip board for small prints and double-weight chip or corrugated board for large sizes. These backing boards are made of wood pulp and chemicals and are not recommended for permanent mounts. Over a period of time the pulp board and backing will discolor the print paper. If a print is to remain in a mounting for a long period of time or is going to be framed, 100% rag mat board and backing is necessary. Museums and reputable galleries use only rag boards for their print collections.

So many oversize prints are now being made that many exhibitions accept them without mats. The exhibiting organizations sometimes require oversize prints to be rolled and provide backing if they are accepted by the jury. Another method sometimes permissible is to back the print with double-weight white mat board cut flush to the size of the print and to wrap a medium-gauge sheet of acetate or clear vinyl around it and tape it from behind. If the double-weight mat board is not heavy enough, corrugated board or some of the new styrofoam boards are excellent because they are rigid and weigh very little; however, they are more expensive.

Measuring the Mat

The size of the mat should not be excessive. Three- to five-inch margins are fairly good as a general rule, with the 3" size for small prints and up to 5" for large prints. We usually make the top and side margins the same width and the bottom an inch larger. The cut-out area of the mat should be about ¼" larger than the print size on top and sides and about ½" larger on the bottom to allow the number, title, and signature to be easily seen.

Start by setting up a clean large measuring and cutting table. The ideal studio space should have a table just for cutting mats and wrapping packages, but that is a luxury of space few artists seem to be able to keep free. Use a large piece of chip board to top the table and to serve as a cutting board. Sharp mat knives and razor blades will soon dull if a hard, rough surface is used for cutting mats. Use a medium pencil with a good long point and do not press hard while marking, or marks may show even after erasing. Use a steel straightedge with a piece of masking tape attached to the underside to keep the straightedge from slipping. Trim both boards to size. Measure and mark off the opening to be cut.

Cutting the Mat

There are many methods for cutting a good, clean, professional mat. The important thing is to find the method that best suits you. Many students come close to hysteria at the thought of cutting a mat. Once the procedure is thought out and simplified, most people should be able to cut a reasonably good mat.

A number of varieties of good mat knives with changeable blades are sold in art supply stores. They are comfortable to hold, but we find the thickness of the blade and the constant need for sharpening a handicap. We prefer single-edge industrial razor blades, 100 to the box, fitted into a sturdy razor-blade holder obtainable in a hardware store. The razor blade is so thin and sharp and cheap that there is no excuse for a dull tool.

We often use two or three blades for one mat. Use the steel ruler as a cutting guide. Some people prefer a steel T-square. Hold down firmly on the ruler or T-square with one hand and cut straight through the board with one stroke to insure an even cut. However, if you don't have the strength for this, two or three careful cuts without moving out of the line will work. Be careful at corners and don't overcut. Some people prefer to mark and cut the mats from the back to avoid erasing and to have better control of corners. It is customary to cut the board at a slight bevel from the edge of the mat and with a little practice this should be possible. Some artists use the slanted side of the steel T-square as a guide, others use mat-cutting devices available in art supply stores.

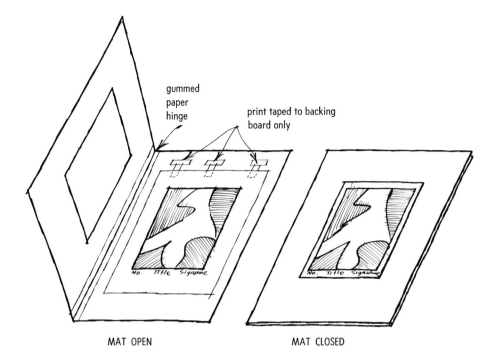

gummed
paper
hinge

print taped to backing
board only

No. Title Signature

No. Title Signature

MAT OPEN   MAT CLOSED

Hinging Mat and Print to Backboard

After the mat is cut, hinge it to the backboard, using gummed linen tape for a permanent mat or gummed paper tape for an impermanent one. Always hinge the longest sides of the mat and backing.

The print is always attached with a hinging device to the backboard, never to the mat. First, position the print carefully with the mat in a closed position, taking care to have even spacing between the print and the edge of the mat. The print should have adequate clean margins so that there will be a sufficient margin area to allow for taping. After the print is positioned, open the mat and attach two strips of gummed linen tape about 2″ in length to the top back of the print, protruding 1″ beyond the print. Place two more strips of gummed linen tape about 3″ in length across the two protruding strips, fastening them securely to the backing. The print now hangs freely from the top only, allowing for the shrinkage and expansion caused by changing dry and humid weather. Strips for hinging may be made from the same paper used for the print. Cut strips from paper scraps and use library paste to adhere the strips to the backing. If a print is large and on heavy paper, three or four hinges might be required, with a spot of Elmer's glue to insure sticking.

Floating the Print

Another method of mounting used widely today, especially for oversized prints, is to float a print on a linen backing for framing. Some artists print their images flush to the edges of their papers, particularly in lithograph and silk-screen prints. The effect can be quite handsome when the deckle of the paper is utilized. Prepared linen boards of actual linen cloth, in a variety of textures and some tones are sold in many art supply stores. Trim the board to the correct size, and place small amounts of Elmer's glue in the two upper back corners and glue it to the backing. The bottom will hang free. The print can then be acetated for shipping to exhibitions or framed for permanence, although the print surface may be damaged by condensation on the inside of the glass.

Acetate or Vinyl Protective Covering

When you send work out to some of the smaller, less well-equipped galleries, it is well to back the prints with a sturdy backing board and to acetate them to protect them from excessive handling in print bins. A good cover is .003 gauge acetate or a clear vinyl wrapped around the print and taped to the backing. The corners can be folded with excess bulk cut away. Acetate can also be trimmed a fraction smaller than the backing and a white tape used to neatly seal the edges.

FRAMING THE PRINT

Framing a print properly is a huge specialized area. There is nothing quite as handsome as professional, first-rate framing. There are many excellent framers, particularly in large cities, and there are framing accommodations in print galleries where the people know prints and can mount and frame them properly. Avoid framers who know nothing of the proper handling of prints because they can do damage. We have seen prints trimmed unmercifully by inept framers to fit a standard mat, and we have also seen one sad job of a print that was dry-mounted to a backing, making the print impossible to remove. Find a reputable framer who specializes in prints, who has a wide selection of framing to choose from, and who will make a dustproof, tightly assembled frame.

One area of print framing that is new and must be dealt with on an individual basis is the framing of dimensional prints. If the structure is paper that has been built up through molding, cutting, or constructing, special frame boxes, usually plexiglas and sometimes glass, must be devised either by the artist himself or with a sympathetic framer. If plexiglas, metal, acetate, mylar, or any other hard nonabsorbent surface is used for the base of the actual print, it can be shown without glazing but will need some kind of mount for hanging or displaying. Vacuum-form printing makes possible a finished product of plastic material that may still be fragile because of the dimensional depth of the projecting image and, if not adequately protected, can crack or crush and be totally ruined.

Glazing

A standard rule for glazing is that work done on paper must be framed under glass to prevent dirt and humidity saturation by the absorbent paper. Any glass unfortunately dulls the image somewhat but is necessary to preserve the work. Avoid glare-proof glass because it distorts the tonal quality of the print. Plexiglas is a good substitute and produces less glare than glass, but unfortunately it is expensive and must be very carefully handled because it scratches easily. Colors fade less under plexiglas than they do under glass.

Metal Section Frames

We have found an easy and less expensive substitute for commercial framing in the metal section frames available in many art supply stores and some bookstores. There are two or three varieties based on similar principles and quite simple to assemble. They are often manufactured in natural aluminum and anodized aluminum that looks golden. The glass must be purchased from a glazier and slipped into the frame.

John Ross
"Sisak" 1966
Collagraph 18" x 30"
Joseph Hirshhorn Collection

THE DEALER AND THE EDITION

As there are many more dealers and distributors who handle prints or purchase individual prints and editions outright than there were 10 years ago, it is much easier now for an artist to find an outlet for selling his work. However, certain pitfalls are worth mentioning. Usually the beginning artist leaves a group of his prints on consignment with the dealer for sale at a specified commission. The percentage that the dealer takes can vary from one third to one half. If the dealer wants your work badly enough, he will sometimes arrange an outright purchase of a number of works at a discounted price. Such a sale can be desirable for the artist in most cases. Distributors of prints will often buy whole editions from an artist at a greatly reduced price, which can vary from 10% or 15% to 30% of the price of the print. The attraction of a large sum of money must be weighed against the time it takes to produce the print.

When an artist leaves work on consignment, he should prepare duplicate sheets with a simply stated agreement specifying amount of commission, his request for monthly payment for work sold, and his request to be able to withdraw his work from the dealer on demand. A listing of prints should then follow, with edition numbers and selling prices. The dealer should be presented with two copies to sign, one for the dealer, one for the artist. Some years ago the Print Council of America, 527 Madison Avenue, New York City, prepared such a form as a guide for artists. It was very useful to us when we began working with numerous dealers.

Investigate all small out-of-town dealers. You can ask for the names of artists handled by the dealer and contact them to inquire about the dealer's working arrangements and general reputation. Remember, it is difficult to retrieve work once it is shipped to distant cities and much easier to do a little investigating before you are involved. Too many artists have suffered badly at the hands of unscrupulous dealers or just from dealers who sold their galleries intact with consignment work to new owners who may or may not be ethical.

RECORD-KEEPING

Unfortunately the very system of edition-making requires some kind of record-keeping. The artist, like the grocery store owner, is dealing with an inventory, and the inventory is his prints. Use the simplest method possible for a very dull job. We generally hate this aspect of printmaking but unfortunately it is necessary. Our system is to keep two large looseleaf notebooks of different colors, one book for noting editions, where sold, where consigned, and the date, and one book to hold agreements and print listings from each gallery, all placed alphabetically (by print titles) in the books. When a print is sold it is checked off in the edition book and in the gallery listing book. This system is fairly accurate. A separate listing of exhibitions where you exhibit each year is also helpful so that a record of the print shown, date and place of show can be made.

SIZE OF EDITION

The handling, signing, numbering, and cataloging of the prints is difficult because the print is produced in a multiple edition. Each print is unique, yet part of a designed quantity of prints called an edition. A similar situation exists in the making of a limited edition of castings by the sculptor; however, such castings are not always numbered.

The printing of the edition itself may be handled in a variety of ways, depending on the probable demand for a print, the ease of printing, and whether the edition is printed by the artist or by a printer for artists. The artist decides on the number to be printed unless a dealer in prints commissions an edition and designates the number for the edition. The usual number for an artist-printed edition used to be 25 or 50. However, so many changes have occurred in the last few years with the appearance of numerous new print galleries and publishers and distributors, coupled with a general increase in demand for prints, that the number of prints in an edition has drastically increased. Editions of 200 to 300 prints are produced quite regularly, and some artists have been known to sign up to 2000 prints, printed by professional artist printers and produced as special editions.

The size of the edition used to be kept small in order to insure the value of each print and hopefully to raise the price of each one as the edition sold out. However, with the wide distribution and demand for the print today it is impossible to speculate on supply and demand in relation to size of edition.

Some artists decide on the size of the edition but do not print the whole number immediately. They may print 10 or 15 to start with, numbering the first group 1 through 15, for an edition of say 50, record the number printed in a book, and then fill out the rest of the edition when they have more printing time or can engage assistants or give out the remainder of the edition to a printer for artists. We often prefer this method for our complicated color collagraphs so that we can be free for new work. A very accurate, detailed printing chart must be kept so that the edition can be filled out exactly as it began. This system has worked very well for us because our diagrams are very good and we supplement them with color saved in wax paper packages and recipes for color mixtures. This method is discussed at length in the chapter on the collagraph.

Other artists prefer to print their whole edition immediately to free themselves from reprinting. Time and experience will determine the method best suited to your work. Of course the deferred-printing system cannot work for lithography or for silk screen. For lithography the stones would be difficult to store, and silk-screen printing is a relatively fast printing technique that allows for fairly easy edition work. Interrupted printing applies best to relief and intaglio printing.

A number of artists feel that the limited-edition numbering system protects only the dealer and the collector at the expense of the artist and refuse to use the system. Instead, they sign the prints and mark them as artist's proofs or only sign them.

When an edition is complete, the blocks, plates, screens, stones, or whatever contains the image should be destroyed or defaced. This precaution against further reproduction is usually requested when editions are commissioned. It is done in many cases by scratching, cutting, or drawing a line through the printing surface. However some unscrupulous dealers have attained possession of plates and then proceeded to print them and sell them unsigned and defaced. Many important 19th- and 20th-century French artists' prints may be found along the Quais in Paris or in small dealer's shops in this condition.

Occasionally an artist prints his edition, retains the blocks or plates, and decides at a later time to pull new prints. The artist may alter his color relationships or perhaps even make structural changes. Any editions pulled from altered blocks or plates should be designated as second editions.

NUMBERING, TITLING, AND SIGNING

The numbering, titling, and signing of the edition has traditionally been done with a medium pencil on the bottom of the print. The number of the print and the size of the edition are written on its lower left side with the designation 1/50 for the first print of an edition of fifty, 2/50 for the second, and so on until 50/50 is numbered. The title is usually written in the bottom center and the artist's signature in the lower right. Whether the edition is printed all at once or over a period of time, the prints should be printed as much the same as possible. The numbering then designates the sequence in time and not prime value for low numbers and less value for higher numbers. Probably the question most asked by laymen is whether print number 1 is more valuable than print number 50. Many artists avoid the whole problem by simply writing edition 50 in the lower left corner of each print. However, the traditional method of individual numbering does afford the artist an accurate bookkeeping device if he sends out many prints to exhibitions.

ARTIST'S PROOFS

Traditionally, 10% of an edition should be designated *artist's proofs*. These prints are of the same quality as the

Jan Krejci
(Czechoslovakia)
"Arnolfini II"
Engraving 7⅞" x 11"
Courtesy of the artist
Photo by Jan Sirovy

numbered edition and are designated as artist's proofs because they are the prints retained by the artist if an entire edition is sold outright or printed and sold one by one. If an edition is sold outright at a discounted price, the artist's proofs will sell at the artist's usual selling price or more, at the discretion of the artist if the edition is sold.

Artist's proofs are also numbered with Roman numerals like I/X and XX/XX or with a system of letters, A, B, C, and so on.

Years ago it was customary for collectors to covet artist's proofs, most often because in the French tradition of print-making the artist worked closely with a printer and inspected the proofs submitted by the printer and marked his choice "bon a tirer" and signed the print as guide for the edition. As these collectors felt this print was the first to meet the artist's approval, it was therefore more desirable. Because artists now print editions themselves and give equal care to the first and the last prints in an edition, this fixation on the artist's proof as the most accurate state has diminished.

WORKING PROOFS

During the early stages of the development of the print the artist may experiment with a number of color combinations, different wipings, or rolling, and the like. Though these prints may not be the final choice for the edition, they often contain many interesting variations and should be marked working proofs and numbered in the sequence pulled. These prints will no doubt have value as an edition is depleted and, more importantly, are of considerable value in studying the development of a print. If you have ever had the opportunity to see the numerous stages of many of Rembrandt's etchings that can be studied, you will understand how interesting the working proofs of an artist can be for the total comprehension of a work of art.

THE RESTRIKE

A restrike is a print that has been pulled from a block or plate at a much later date than the original printing. Many restrikes exist of Rembrandt etchings, pulled in the 18th and 19th centuries. Numerous restrike prints exist of work by Goya and Kollwitz. Such impressions may be inferior to the prints printed in the artist's lifetime. Sometimes the plates are reworked, usually being steel-faced in order to obtain long runs. When the prints are sold as restrikes at modest prices they are often interesting to study and to own. When the restrikes are sold as artist-pulled proofs for large sums, it is most unfortunate for the unsuspecting buyer. The best advice in this area would be to always buy from a reputable dealer and be wary of "fantastic" buys in master prints. Finding such a buy is highly unlikely.

Vladimir Gażoviċ
(Czechoslovakia)
"Susanah and the Elders" 1970
Etching
Courtesy of the artist

Käthe Kollwitz
"Weavers Cycle: March of the Weavers"
Etching 8" x 11½"
Collection of the authors

COLLECTING PRINTS

The burgeoning interest in the fine print has caused many artists to explore printmaking techniques. It has spurred galleries to exhibit and commission new prints for a new generation of print collectors. It has prompted museums to mount survey and retrospective exhibitions of contemporary and historic prints. And, to exploit this renaissance, print dealers, agents and wholesalers have sprung up like mushrooms all over the country. The print has many lovers, and new processes and techniques follow each other with increasing rapidity. It is a complex scene which greets the collector who has become intrigued by the print.

What Is An Original Print?

Definitions which once seemed to be complete, final, and absolute only a decade ago now seem ambiguous and unclear. An original print was described in a brochure issued by the Print Council in 1961 as a work of graphic art, the general requirements of which are:

1. The artist alone has made the image in or upon the plate, stone, wood block, or other material, for the purpose of creating a work of graphic art.

2. The impression is made directly from the original material by the artist or pursuant to his directions.

3. The finished print is approved by the artist.

This is still a helpful definition but it does not cover many of the situations which are arising now. The modern methods of printing, particularly in offset lithography and screen printing, have offered artists ways to create images and textures that have not been attainable in prior years.

Photographic methods that were considered reproductive are now being used by artists, with the help of skilled technicians from the commercial printing plants that abound in our mass-communicators society. Museums are accepting as original prints those impressions which would have been rejected ten or twenty years ago. The press-printed lithograph or silkscreen can be turned out in editions of thousands, and some galleries are offering color lithos in signed editions of from 3000 to 10,000 impressions. *Art in America* has printed 60,000 impressions of photographically prepared plates which are claimed to be original prints. The addition of the artist's signature is said to make the impression 100 times more valuable!

It is difficult to tell a photo-lithographic reproduction from an original lithograph, especially when the reproduction is printed on fine rag paper and has a pencilled number and a forged signature in the corner. Even well-known artists succumb to the temptation of ready cash and let craftsmen interpret watercolors, drawings and other art work into the print media. Sometimes these prints are carefully supervised by the artist but often they are not. When another artist or craftsman redraws the image on to a stone or plate the resulting print often changes in character and may distort the original drawing or design. An ethical practice would dictate that the artist-designer and the craftsman both be identified as having created the print. Some artists have been known to sign blank paper in advance of the printing of the edition. Eventually these practices will cause the discriminating collector to re-examine the prints offered for sale, with an eye to quality of impression, the strength of the image, and the size of the edition. All of these factors, plus the reputation of the artist, enter into the pricing of the print.

The print market, which in the 60's seemed to be insatiable, was affected by the general economic recession of 1970–71 and sales dropped considerably. Many galleries retrenched, some went out of business and prices of some contemporary artists either leveled off or went down. The market for old master prints held up quite well, however, and these prints are still demanding very high prices, with masterpiece prints by Rembrandt and Goya exceeding prices in six figures. The print market will undoubtedly be responsive to new changes in business and economic conditions.

Should The Collector Specialize?

The cost of amassing a good general collection of prints, with first-rate examples of great masters, is so high that only the rich can attempt it. Most people will be attracted to a certain period, or to a style, or even to an individual artist whose work they admire. A collector can restrict his interest to a single country, to a certain type of image which has special meaning to him, or in any manner which satisfies his desire to collect. Some people acquire prints as an investment against the seemingly perpetual inflation which erodes the value of currency. Certainly it is more rewarding from an esthetic point of view to study the etchings and engravings of the masters than those rather formal portraits of the presidents on paper money. The art work seems to have better durability than the cash!

In order to understand the area in which you collect it is vital to acquire some knowledge in the field. This means that the collector should first collect a few books or catalogs which describe the prints which interest him. There are catalogue raisonne's which list the entire production of an artist over his life-span. These are helpful to a serious collector who needs to know details of states and editions. Many print dealers issue catalogs which describe the prints being offered

Clare Romano
"New Jersey Landscape I" 1968
Collagraph 23½" x 24"

for sale. When prices are listed these catalogs form a record of print values over the years which can be fascinating (or frustrating) to collectors. The Print Collector's Newsletter 205 East 78th Street, New York, New York 10021, is published as a bimonthly brochure in looseleaf format which gives latest prices and information on new editions of original prints. It also lists upcoming auction sales of prints as a service to its subscribers.

The way to learn about prints is to study them, find an area that interests you and then pursue that area, looking at as many prints as you can. You will then know what books and catalogs will help you in your search. If a workshop class in printmaking is available it will be helpful for the collector to enroll in order to better understand the diverse techniques which are used by artists. Many colleges and art schools offer evening courses in printmaking on a non-matriculated basis, some taught by respected and productive artists.

Where To Find Prints

Dealers have appeared all over the country. Some have elaborate gallery facilities, others operate from a closet in the hall. Some know a great deal, others know very little. A reputable, established dealer is the best source for continued acquisition of prints, of course, but sometimes a good print will appear in a gift shop, or in a decorator's boutique, or in a furniture store. When this happens, you must rely on your own knowledge and judgment as to current values. Despite recent history, print values cannot constantly go up. Therefore you should be as informed as possible in order to protect yourself from ambitious dealers or overpriced editions. Many larger companies send traveling salesmen on the road with thousands of prints, covered with acetate or vinyl, to mount one-day sales in such places as college or university galleries, libraries, or schools. Many of these exhibits contain excellent prints, but they usually include some restrikes (impressions from a plate pulled without the approval of the artist, usually after his death). There is nothing wrong with restrikes so long as they are labeled as such and it is clearly understood what they are. The general public could not afford a Durer, Goya, Rembrandt, Callot or Kollwitz if the plates were not reprinted many times. Variations in price between early and late printings of the same plate can be enormous because the plates wear rapidly, especially delicate areas such as aquatint or drypoint. Early printings have the richest blacks and the strongest tonality.

John Ross
"Boulevard" 1964
Collagraph 16¼" x 26¾"

Some prints being offered for sale are cut from old magazines, such as "Verve," which were printed in very large editions (often in the thousands). These prints may be technically "originals" but should be priced accordingly.

It may be possible to buy work directly from a living artist, when you are in his neighborhood. Some artists will be distracted by this, however, and their work may be obtained only from their dealers. The most direct contact is usually the best, with the least amount of "handling" and "wholesaling" producing the best guarantee of authenticity and often the lowest prices.

A few print societies publish prints of contemporary artists, usually at favorable prices. These prints are normally restricted to members but often membership in these groups is a simple matter of joining and paying an annual fee. The Society of American Graphic Artists (S.A.G.A.) at 1083 Fifth Avenue, New York, New York 10028, offers prints by its distinguished artist members to its associate members at very low prices. The International Graphic Arts Society (I.G.A.S.) at 410 East 62nd Street, New York, New York, 10021, also offers editions of especially commissioned prints to its membership at prices much less than normal. The Print Club of Philadelphia, 1614 Latimer Street, Philadelphia, Pennsylvania, has been active in the field for many years and publishes small editions of prints, with a preferential price to its members. Many other non-profit societies and groups offer prints to a select group, usually at a distinct price advantage over the normal commercial channels.

Many museums offer prints to the public which are not available through commercial galleries or dealers. The sponsoring institution can not guarantee the immortality of any of its selections but, as the panel which chooses the print to be published is likely to be composed of experts the chances are that their choice will have some validity, at least.

Auctions and special sales are usually publicized in local newspapers. These may contain many worthwhile impressions but the buyer is completely on his own, as items purchased can rarely be returned. A collector may locate other collectors who will either sell or trade prints in order to build a collection in a certain field. Many publishers are releasing portfolios and deluxe volumes of illustrated books which contain fine prints, usually at a reasonable price because of the number of prints involved. The collecting of fine books which contain original prints is an area which combines literature and the visual arts in a particularly satisfying way.

How To Show and Store Prints

Most collectors display only a portion of their treasures on the walls. Like the tip of an iceberg, these may just indicate the bulk of the work stored in cabinets or closets. Color prints, especially, should be displayed only in subdued light, preferably away from reflected sunlight, and should not be left on display for extended periods of time. All colors will eventually change if exposed to bright light. The careful collector will be content to view his most brilliant color pieces at intervals.

Prints should touch only 100% rag mounts and should be hung from the back portion of the mount with non-staining

Prints can be stored vertically or horizontally in Romano-Ross workshop. Shelves are spaced three to six inches apart.

Permanent storage of prints can be obtained by using solander cases, with dust proof lids and spring catches.

hinges. Cardboard mats are not necessary, except for very large prints (over 30″) because they bulk up the collection and take up too much room. Heavy paper will suffice for most prints of small and medium size. These may be stored flat in solander cases, which are dustproof and have positive spring latches to close the lid. Portfolios are good when they have flaps to keep out dust and if they are closed tightly to prevent warping. They are not as good as solander cases for long term storage.

When prints are to be displayed on walls, they should be covered with glass to protect them from dust and dirt. The edges of the glass should be protected by a frame and the back sealed. The surface of the print should not touch the glass because condensation on the inside of the frame might cause water staining. This can be achieved with a suitable mat or strips to separate the print from the glass.

Patented brackets and other devices are good for temporary display of prints and should not be used as permanent fixtures. Dimensional prints need special boxes, often made of plastic, which scratches from the continual cleaning necessary to keep the dust away. Sheet plastic has a curious magnetic quality which attracts dust. Very large prints are difficult to store and need large cabinets or strong crates to keep them. Some may be rolled and kept in cardboard tubes. As a collection grows it may need its own room, which should have a large work table, good general illumination, and a movable small lamp for close examination of prints. A magnifying glass of 8 or 10 power is a help when studying some prints.

THE PRINT WORKSHOP

INTRODUCTION

The activities of the printmaking workshop are quite specialized and require careful organization and purchase of equipment to ensure an efficient, productive setup. It is possible to use one room for more than one process, but it is rarely possible to equip a shop for all the techniques (etching, lithography, relief printing, and screen printing) unless the room is larger than 1800 or 2000 square feet. A one-man studio can be slightly smaller but not much, because the presses and storage racks take up large amounts of space. It is better to have separate rooms for etching and lithography, although relief printing and screen printing can be accomplished on sturdy tables in almost any room large enough to hold them. When a number of printmakers work together it is wise to limit the number of techniques to two or three, particularly in a school or teaching situation. Screen printing takes a tremendous amount of table space, and each printer needs his own drying rack to accommodate the rapid flow of prints. Etching workshops need the smallest amount of space, while the relief print needs the least amount of expensive equipment, if prints are to be printed by hand rubbing and a press is not used.

THE ROOM

Although the size of a printmaking workshop can vary greatly, it should not be less than 800 to 1000 square feet if paper is stored in the room. The handling of paper requires a clean table, and this area must be kept away from the ink, acids, and other chemicals used in the workshop. Each additional artist requires about 40 to 50 square feet of workspace. The number of people working in a shop should not exceed 16 to 20, with 10 a much more workable number.

The light values in a print workshop should be fairly high. The general level of illumination should not fall below an exposure value of 10. A good photographic exposure meter will check this reading when held about one foot from a sheet of white paper in the work area of the room. Storage

Taira checks a proof at Desjobert's. Note that old litho stones are used for inking slabs.

areas can have less light, but press and drawing areas may be slightly higher. Fluorescent lighting will be the most efficient way of achieving these levels at night. Use cool-white tubes for the best color balance. In the daytime the light that comes from the north is best. If the light comes from another direction, shades or venetian blinds should be available to control direct sunlight. Air conditioning is almost an essential in most of the United States in the summer. Not only will people work more efficiently in an air-conditioned room, but paper and ink will not dry too quickly in the heat of the day. Printmaking is occasionally a strenuous activity, especially when you are graining a litho stone or wiping a collagraph, and a cool studio is better than a warm one. Ideal temperatures in a workshop will range between 65° and 68° Fahrenheit.

The walls of the workshop may be made of Homasote wallboard, a composition that makes excellent bulletin board material to which prints can be pinned or stapled. Ceilings and walls should be painted white or grey, with no strong colors that might affect the colors in a print. The floor can be painted concrete, asphalt tile, linoleum tile, or wood. Slate makes an excellent floor. Wood should be varnished or shellacked to make sweeping simple. Certain chemicals, such as ether ground, will dissolve asphalt tile, acid spills should be mopped up quickly; the shop should be kept clean and neat. Printmaking is a messy business, at best, and the struggle for cleanliness is unending. Brooms and dustpans should be available and cleaning the shop should be a daily ritual.

EQUIPMENT

A well-equipped printmaking workshop will include one or two etching presses, a lithographic hand press, and a proof press for relief prints, such as a Vandercook. These presses may each weigh a ton or more; and if the floor supports are not strong enough, the weight of a press may be distributed over a larger area by placing it on two wooden 4 by 4's or two sheets of ¾" plywood as additional supports under the legs of the press. A good etching press with a bed 24" wide will cost $2000 or more. A litho press will be approximately the same or a little more. A used 219 Vandercook press will cost $2500 or more, depending upon condition.

At least one large sink is necessary. It may be made of stone, stainless steel, or porcelain, although porcelain is less desirable. A large shallow sink is better than a deep small sink. A litho graining table may be built into a large sink, in which case some arrangement should be made to prevent large amounts of sludge from clogging the drain.

A good, sharp paper cutter is necessary. It should be at least 30" square, and 36" is better. There must be a number of solidly built work tables in the shop. The folding type of table is simply not strong enough to take heavy litho stones and other printmaking procedures common to all workrooms. Mounting the tables on heavy-duty industrial casters will be a great convenience if the room arrangement is to be changed.

Acid and water trays are essential. They should be made of stainless steel with built-in spigots or of plastic material

An acid cabinet at Indiana University. The glass panel slides down when long, deep bites are taking place. The vent hood should be made of stainless steel for long life. Acid fumes are corrosive and dangerous.

The "library" of small stones at Desjobert's workshop.

like that used in photo darkrooms. These trays should be near the sink for easy wash-up and drainage.

Litho stones can be moved easily on a wheeled cart made from a small, strong table fitted with industrial casters. A fork-lift truck is required for large stones that weigh over 150 pounds.

A number of inking slabs will be used in the workshop. These can be made from ¼" plate glass mounted on top of strong tables. White cardboard should be placed under the glass, and the glass then fixed into position with wood strips or strapping tape. Old litho stones or marble slabs make good inking surfaces. As formica will eventually scratch, it is less desirable, but it may be used. Stiff palette knives are also needed; and these should be stored near the inking slabs.

The amount of trash that accumulates during a day's printmaking is astounding. Several large wastepaper containers should be available. At least one covered, fireproof waste can is needed for old inking rags and cleaning rags. Do not use turpentine in the workshop. It may cause spontaneous combustion if rags soaked in it are packed into a waste can.

Drying racks for paper are needed in a screen-printing shop. These may be made in various ways, but all should be on wheels for easy mobility. A good hotplate is necessary; and a separate electric line, perhaps of 220 volts, may be needed to accommodate a large hotplate. Other items helpful in some shops are plastic siphons for draining acids, staple guns for attaching prints to walls, hammers, screw drivers, files, rulers, straight-edges, T-squares, triangles, and the like.

STORAGE IN THE PRINT SHOP

Paper should be stored in the original wrapper even after the package has been slit open and sheets are being removed. Avoid touching the paper until absolutely necessary. The cost of quality paper is very high, and each wasted sheet is an expense that is hard to justify. Have assistants or monitors handle the paper in a school shop and sell it to the students. Keep paper in flat blueprint files. Old wooden files are cheap but not so good as metal cabinets with roller bearings. Large quantities of paper can be stored flat on ¾″ plywood shelves. Newsprint can be purchased by the ream in several sizes (18″ by 24″ and 24″ by 36″ are convenient). Index paper and cover stock should be bought in cartons, usually by weight; 500 sheets is the normal carton. Tableau paper can be purchased in rolls for large prints and in cut sizes for smaller prints (24″ by 36″ is good). A roll of kraft wrapping paper is

Frasconi, in his South Norwalk studio, with a book-binding press, his inking table and work table.

Intaglio inking area at Bank Street Atelier. Convenient storage of inks and chemicals and good lighting (both natural and artificial) commend this workshop.

a good item to keep in the shop. Corrugated board in 36″ by 48″ flat pieces is useful for backing and for general packaging. It should be purchased from a commercial supplier in quantity and needs a large area for storage.

Ink, plate oil, chemicals, and paints should be stored in shallow wall cabinets for ease of access. Deep cabinets are hard to stock, and it is difficult to see what is in the rear. Acids should be kept in cabinets with doors and locks to prevent unauthorized usage. In New York City, nitric acid is considered a weapon, and its sale to unauthorized persons is discouraged. If the shop services 20 or more printmakers, mineral spirits should be purchased in 55-gallon drums and then siphoned into gallon safety containers. Lacquer thinner, alcohol, adhering fluid, shellac, and other solvents should be kept in covered metal containers.

Racks can be constructed from 2′ by 4′ verticals with ¾″ plywood shelves for litho stones (shelves should have horizontal 2″ by 4″ stringers underneath for support). Zinc plates for litho and etching should be stored flat on plywood shelves. A school might want to lock up certain items, such as paper and plates, because of their high cost. Silk-screen inks, which are used in quart cans for certain colors and in gallon cans for extender and transparent base, require a large amount of storage space. Screens may be stored in overhead racks with vertical dividers every 8″ or so.

Finished prints should be kept in metal blueprint-file cabinets. In schools, each student could be assigned a drawer for his completed prints. In the private workshop, boxes or solander cases may be used to store completed editions before they are shipped to galleries and exhibitions.

VENTILATION AND ELECTRICITY

Acid fumes should be vented to the outside by an electric fan with the ductwork and vents made of stainless steel or of galvanized steel painted with asphaltum paint. Fumes from solvents used in screen printing are very toxic and should be vented efficiently. Spray paints used in aquatints are particularly harmful and should be used outdoors or in very well ventilated areas. Cellar rooms with small windows are a poor choice for print-making workshops.

Electric hotplates may require 220-volt lines if two or more are needed. One hotplate will function on a 110-volt line if it is on a separate circuit. Outlets should be liberally placed throughout the workshop because electric hand tools are very useful in a busy shop. Grinders, routers, polishers,

The acid room at Pratt Institute in Brooklyn. Different strengths of acid should be clearly labeled.

saws, and sanders are being used in more and more workshops. Motorized presses need electric power. Table lamps are helpful when high-intensity light is needed, and they need power, too. A radio is frequently welcome, especially while printing editions.

PHOTOGRAPHIC EQUIPMENT

A well-equipped professional or college printmaker's studio will have facilities for making positive transparencies and for exposing them on to screens, plates, or stones. The most expensive piece of equipment is a large process camera, which will cost about $2,000 in the 14″ by 17″ size. This camera will need its own darkroom with sink and running water. A carbon arc lamp with a vacuum table for exposing the plate will cost about $600 for a 22″ by 28″ unit. Although photoflood lamps make a workable substitute, a high volume of work may make the cost of a vacuum table a good investment as it cuts the exposure time by a considerable amount. The popularity of photo images and techniques is increasing rapidly, and many schools and shops are purchasing this equipment.

SAFETY MEASURES

Every workshop must have at least one (preferably more) fire extinguisher of the chemical foam type. They should be checked regularly to insure their workability. A first aid kit is also essential, including antiseptics, bandaids, bandages, and burn lotion.

Robert Blackburn's Printmaking Workshop in New York City has five geared etching presses, and two lithograph presses.

Many large diameter rollers are used in Blackburn's shop for relief and intaglio prints. They are stored in notched racks.

SOURCES AND CHARTS

SOURCES OF SUPPLIES FOR PRINTMAKING

General Supplies (tools, paper, ink, and so on)

Craftool Company
1 Industrial Road
Woodridge, New Jersey 07075

Sam Flax
25 East 28 Street
New York, New York 10016
(Also in Chicago, Los Angeles, San Francisco, and Sacramento)

Arthur Brown
2 West 46 Street
New York, New York

Fine Arts Materials Co.
531 LaGuardia Place
New York, New York

Rembrandt Graphic Arts Co.
Stockton, New Jersey 08559

F. Weber Co. (order from local dealers)
Wayne and Windrim Avenue
Philadelphia, Pennsylvania 19144

Graphic Chemical & Ink Co.
P. O. Box 27
728 North Yale Avenue
Villa Park, Illinois 60181

Tools (gouges, knives, chisels, stones, and so on)

E. C. Lyons
16 West 22 Street
New York, New York 10011

E. C. Mueller
3646 White Plains Road
Bronx, New York 10467

Wilfred C. Kimber, Ltd.
24 King's Bench Street
Blackfriars
London, S.E.1, England
(also Hunter, Penrose, Littlejohn Ltd.

Felt Blankets

Continental Felt Co.
22 West 15th Street
New York, New York

Pacific States Felt & Mfg. Co.
843 Howard Street
San Francisco, California 94103

Pigments (for ink and paint):

Fezandie & Sperrle Inc.
103 Lafayette Street
New York, New York 10013

Interchemical Printing Corp.
16th and Willow
Oakland, California

E. I. DuPont De Nemours Co.
Pigments Department
Wilmington, Delaware

Acids and Chemicals:

Amend Drug and Chemical Co.
83 Cordier Street
Irvington, New Jersey

City Chemical Co.
132 West 22 St.
New York, New York

Philip Hunt Co.
707 Army Street
San Francisco, California 94124
for Gentry Clove Oil:
Beacon Chemical Co.
244 Lafayette Street
New York, N. Y. 10012

Photoengraving Supplies, Including Copper and Zinc Plates:

Harold Pitman Co.
515 Secaucus Road
Secaucus, New Jersey 07094

For small quantities:
National Steel & Copper Plate Co.
653 10th Avenue
New York, N. Y.

Bond Metal Supply Co.
321 Canal Street
New York, N. Y.

Rollers and Brayers:

Apex Roller Co.
1541 No. 16 Street
St. Louis, Missouri

Ideal Roller Co.
21 39th Avenue
Long Island City, New York

Jomac, Inc.
181 Broad Street
Carlstadt, New Jersey

Speedball Soft Rubber Brayers
Hunt Manufacturing Co.
Statesville, North Carolina
(Many local dealers)

Cylinder Rubber (for rollers):

Miller Products Co.
29 Warren Street
New York, New York

Printing Ink (letterpress):

IPI (Interchem Corp.) (Everyday Ink)
636 11 Avenue
New York, New York

Siebold Ink Co.
150 Varick Street
New York, New York

Sun Chemical Corp.
General Printing Ink
750 3rd Avenue
New York, New York 10017

Ink (intaglio):

Cronite Company
88th Street & Kennedy Blvd.
North Bergen, New Jersey

(also Graphic Chemical & Ink Co.

F. Charbonnel
13 Quai Montebello
Paris, Veme, France

Lorilleux-Lefranc & Co.
16 Rue Suger
Paris, VIeme, France

Usher-Walker Ltd.
Chancery House
Chancery Lane
London, W.C.2, England

Crinoline or Tarletan:

in large quantities only (100 yds. or more)
Gross-Kobrick
370 West 35th Street
New York, New York

A & S Textile Co., Inc.
236 West 27th Street
New York, N. Y.

Paper:

large stock of imported and domestic papers:
Andrews/Nelson/Whitehead
7 Laight Street (on Canal St.)
New York, New York 10013

for white index and cover stock:
Crestwood Paper Corp.
263 9th Avenue
New York, New York

cover stock, blotters
Saxon Paper Co.
240 West 18th Street
New York, New York

Corrugated board in quantity:
Standard Corrugated & Case Corp.
686 Grand Avenue
Ridgefield, N. J. 07657

West coast dealer for A/N/W
Zellerbach Paper Co.
234 South Spruce Street
South San Francisco, California 94118

Mat, chipboard in quantity:
Miller Cardboard Co.
80–82 Wooster Street
New York, New York

for blotters, commercial cover stock:
Lindenmeyer, Schlosser Corp.
5301 11th Street
New York, New York

Photographic Techniques

For Kodak KPR Chemicals & Ortho Film:
Treck Photographic Inc.
1 West 39th Street
New York, New York 10018

For Print-E-Mulsion & SC 12 Superfast:
Rockland Colloid Corp.
599 River Road
Piermont, New York 10968

For Lacquer Toppings (grounds):
Teaneck Chemical Co.
197 Washington Avenue
Carlstadt, New Jersey

Plastic Sheets

Commercial Plastic & Supply Corp.
630 Broadway
New York, New York
or local supplier

Benelux Press Beds

Laminated Sheet Products
Industrial Park Corporation
Norwood, Massachussetts

Hard Ground (mixed with lacquer thinner)

Heims Etching Ground
John L. Heim
1205 Virginia Avenue
Glendale 2, Calif.
(Available from Cronite Co.)

Steel Facing of Copper Plates

Anderson & Lamb
Fulton Street
Brooklyn, New York

CANADIAN SUPPLIERS

Artist's Supplies, Papers, Inks

Heinz Jordan & Co., Ltd.
42 Gladstone Ave.
Toronto 3, Ontario, Canada

Inks

E. Harris Co., Ltd.
1397 Odlum Drive
Vancouver, British Columbia

Chemicals

Christie Chemical Co.
7995 14th Avenue, St. Michel
Montreal 455, Quebec, Canada

Fine Papers

Coast Paper
798 Beatty Street
Vancouver, British Columbia

Etching Press

Zimmcor Artmetwork, Inc.
6120 Metropolitan East
Montreal 451, Quebec, Canada

BOOKS ON PHOTO TECHNIQUES

Kodak Diazo Litho Plate D; Exposing, Processing, and Handling

Publication Q-50
Eastman Kodak Company
Rochester, New York 14650

An Introduction to Photofabrication using Kodak Photosensitive Resists-P-79 (for intaglio & relief), also P-125
Department 454
Eastman Kodak Company
Rochester, New York 14650

PAPERS FOR PRINTMAKING

Name	Size (in.)	Composition	Intaglio	Litho	Relief	Silk Screen	Notes
American Etching	38 x 50	100% rag, machine-made.	x	x		x	Large size for intaglio plates. White, soft finish, prints well.
Arches Cover	22 x 30 / 29 x 41	90% rag, mould-made.	x	x	x	x	Available in white and buff; smooth, even, beautiful texture. Handsome finish.
Arches Text	25 x 40	90% rag, mould-made.	x	x	x	x	Light, even, white, laid and wove finish.
Basingwerk Heavy	26 x 40	45% Esparto pulp, machine-made.	x	x	x	x	Very smooth, even surface. Good for proofs. Inexpensive, useful paper.
Beckett Cover	26 x 40	25% rag, machine-made.	x	x	x	x	Inexpensive, smooth, brilliant white permanent paper, very useful.
Classico Watercolor	22 x 30	100% rag, mould-made.	x				Beautiful, heavy, handsome, white, textured, expensive, for intaglio prints.
Copperplate	22 x 30 / 30 x 42	33% rag, mould-made.	x	x		x	Soft, white. Fragile when damp and should be handled with care. Prints well.
Copperplate Deluxe	22 x 30 / 30 x 42	75% rag, mould-made.	x	x		x	Permanent, white, soft, needs little dampening to soften fibres, expensive.
Crisbrook Etching	22 x 31	100% rag, handmade.	x	x		x	Soft, white, unsized. Prints well. Fairly expensive.
Domestic Etching	26 x 40	50% rag, machine-made.	x	x	x	x	Cheap, white, useful paper.
English Etching	22 x 31	100% rag, mould-made.	x	x	x	x	White, nice texture, moderately priced, handsome sheet.
German Etching	22 x 30 / 30 x 42	75% rag, mould-made.	x	x	x	x	Beautiful finish, soft, white, even, moderately expensive.
Goyu	21 x 29	Part Kozo, handmade.		x		x	Thin, off-white, even texture. Prints delicate detail well.
Hosho	19 x 24	Part Kozo, handmade.		x	x	x	White, soft, small sheet, good for color woodcuts. Picks up fluff on press.
Hosho (student)	16 x 22	Part Kozo, handmade.			x	x	Cheap, uneven, small, good for student proofs.
Hosho Pure	—	Part Kozo, handmade.		x	x	x	Expensive, beautiful, strong off-white handsome sheet. Available only from Japan.
Index	26 x 40	100% sulphite pulp, machine-made.	x	x	x	x	Cheap proof paper. Strong, white, turns brittle with age.
Inomachi (Nacre)	20 x 26	100% Kozo, handmade.	x	x	x	x	Elegant threaded texture. Prints etchings well but must be carefully dampened. Expensive.
Italia	20 x 28 / 28 x 40	67% rag, mould-made.	x	x	x	x	White, soft, handsome finish. Moderately priced. Does not erase well.
Iyo Glazed	17 x 22	Part Kozo, handmade.			x	x	Uneven texture, white, small sheet, inexpensive.
J. Green Watercolor	27 x 40	100% rag, mould-made.	x	x		x	Nice texture, warm white, prints well, handsome sheet.
Kizuki-bosho	17 x 24 / 25 x 35	100% Kozo, handmade.			x	x	Sized on both sides, for Japanese method with water-based inks. Made by same family for seven generations.

Name	Size	Composition				Description
Kochi	20 x 26	Part Kozo, handmade.		x	x	Warm off-white, handsome finish, elegant look, moderately priced, uneven thickness.
Masa 225	21 x 31	Manila and sulphite, machine-made.		x	x	Cheap, flecked, natural color, good for black-and-white proofs. Not permanent.
Millbourn 140 lb.	22 x 30	100% rag, handmade.	x		x	Expensive, beautiful, lovely texture. Strong white. A handsome sheet.
Mohawk Text	26 x 40	100% sulphite, machine-made.	x	x	x	Cheap, proving paper only.
Moriki 1009	25 x 36	Kozo, handmade			x	White, soft, unsized, useful paper.
Moriki (colors)	25 x 36	Kozo, handmade		x	x	Many beautiful colors. Soft, unsized, moderately priced.
Mulberry	24 x 33	Part Kozo, handmade.		x	x	Thin, off-white, tears easily. Not expensive. Good for general woodcut printing.
Mulberry Student	24 x 33	Sulphite, handmade.		x	x	Cheap paper for proofs and student work.
Murillo	27 x 39	33% rag, mould-made.	x		x	Very heavy, strong, buff color, even texture, good for deep intaglio and very sensitive.
Okawara	36 x 72	Kozo, handmade.		x	x	Very large, natural tan color, fairly opaque, even texture, handsome finish.
Opaline Parchment	22 x 28	100% sulphite, machine-made.		x	x	Smooth, even finish. Good for wood engravings and delicate relief prints. Discolors.
Pericles Cover	26 x 40	Rag and sulphite, machine-made.	x	x	x	Fairly permanent, white, smooth, even, good for silk-screen editions.
Rives Heavy	19 x 26 / 26 x 40	100% rag, mould-made.	x	x	x	White, slight texture, not heavy enough for deep embossing, but very useful.
Rives BFK	22 x 30 / 29 x 41	100% rag, mould-made.	x	x	x	A standard paper with many uses. White, even smooth texture, almost opaque. A classic paper.
Sekishu	24 x 39	Kozo, handmade.		x	x	Two colors available, white and natural, thin, soft, inexpensive, tears easily.
Strathmore Artists	—	100% rag, machine-made.	x	x	x	Strong, white sheet with monotonous texture.
Suzuki	36 x 72	Part Kozo, handmade.			x	Very large, white, slight texture. Good for large woodcuts, medium weight.
Tableau	40" rolls	Machine-made.		x	x	Unlimited length, very tough, will not discolor, used as a filter paper. Available in cut sheets.
Torinoko	21 x 31	Part manila hemp.		x	x	Strong, white, opaque, expensive, nice texture.
Troya #40	24 x 36	Hemp, machine-made.		x	x	Cheap, smooth, even paper, good for proofs. Will discolor to pale brown, turns brittle with age.
Tuscan Cover	26 x 40	100% sulphite, machine-made.	x	x	x	Good for etching proofs, is cheap, smooth, turns brittle with age.

Note: Esparto is a grass fiber. Kozo is a plant fiber.

ETCHING PRESSES, Domestic Currently Available

Manufacturer	Bed Size	Gears	Weight	Micrometers Available	Price*	Motor Available	Comments
Charles Brand 84 East 10 St. New York, N.Y. 10003	12 x 24	No	90	No	295	No	Well-made, highly respected machines custom-made to your order.
	16 x 30	Yes	350	Yes	795	No	
	18 x 36	6:1	760	Yes	1460	Yes	
	22 x 24	6:1	880	Yes	1770	Yes	
	24 x 46	6:1	970	Yes	1890	Yes	
	26 x 48	6:1	1100	Yes	1995	Yes	
	30 x 50	6:1	1300	Yes	2310	Yes	
	36 x 60	6:1	1900	Yes	2930	Yes	
Sturges Graphic Chem. P.O. Box 27 Villa Park Illinois 60181	18 x 48	9:1	290	Yes	480	Yes	Solid, sturdy, slow.
	28 x 48	9:1	1300	Yes	1375	No	
Dickerson Combination (from Graphic Chemical Co.)	27 x 48	Yes	400	No	985	Included	Motorized rollers must be shielded.
Craftool Co. Woodridge New Jersey 07075	12 x 24	Yes	61	No	160	No	Complicated mechanism.
	14 x 20	Yes	242	No	450	No	
	18 x 30	Yes	395	No	575	No	
	24 x 40	Yes	—	No	1450	No	
	24 x 40	No	1240	No	1950	No	
Rembrandt Graphic Arts Co. Stockton, N.J. 08559	16 x 32	No	—	No	270	No	This company also sells used presses when available. Many models.
	24 x 42	3:1	1200	Yes	1530	Yes	
	28 x 48	7:1	1200	Yes	1650	Yes	
	30 x 50	7:1	1200	Yes	1950	Yes	
Sam Flax 25 East 28 St. New York, N.Y. 10016	10 x 18	No	50	No	115	Yes	Small presses only.
	13 x 25	Yes	77	No	175	Yes	
	17 x 33	Yes	260	No	650	Yes	
	19 x 29	Yes	550	No	900	Yes	
Meeker-McFee 309 Parkway Madison Wisconsin	25 x 48	120:1	400	Included	1600	Included	An unusual frame design. A solid press.
Glen Alps 6523 40th Ave. N.E. Seattle Wash. 98115	40 x 66	60:1	2850	No	2600	Included	Heavy, strong, large presses.
	28 x 66		2000	No	2000	No	

Maker / Address	Size	Geared	Price	Stand	Price	Stand	Motorized	Comments
Griffin Co. 2241 Sixth St. Berkeley Calif. 94710	24 x 40	Yes	500	No	—	No	No	A new design.
	30 x 50	Yes	700	No	—	No	No	
F. Weber Co. Wayne & Windrim Aves. Philadelphia, Pa. 19144	10 x 18	No	50	No	150	No	No	Small presses only.
	13 x 25	Yes	77	No	225	No	No	
American-French Tool Co. Route 117 Coventry, Rhode Island 02816	24 x 48	4:1	1845	No	1685	No	No	Simple, well-built machines.
	30 x 52	4:1	2115	No	1985	No	No	
	36 x 60	4:1	2420	No	2285	No	No	
Craftsmen Machinery Co. 75 W. Dedham St. Boston, Mass. 02118	24 x 48	26:1	485	Included	1200	Included	No	Easily taken apart for travelling.
William Crull 155 South Lakeshore Rd. Lakeside, Mich. 49116	24 x 36	12:1	1200	Included	1400	Included	No	
	30 x 48	12:1	1450	Included	1750	Included	No	
	36 x 60	12:1	1800	Included	2250	Included	No	
Martech P.O. Box 36 Northport, New York, 11768	12 x 24	Yes		No	275	No	Yes	Motorizing $300 extra. Many good features.
	16 x 30	Yes		No	750	No	Yes	
	18 x 36	Yes		No	1400	No	Yes	
	20 x 40	Yes		No	1600	No	Yes	
	24 x 46	Yes		No	1850	No	Yes	
	28 x 50	Yes		No	2050	No	Yes	
	30 x 50	Yes		No	2300	No	Yes	
	36 x 60	Yes		No	2900	No	Yes	
Product Design Corporation 18 Marshall St. Norwalk, Conn. 06856	32 x 48	25 tons	2500	No	3240	No	Yes	Vertical pressure by hydraulic system. Good for deep embossing. Not a normal geared press.
	32 x 48	50 tons	3300	No	4260	No	Yes	

*Prices are changing constantly, usually upwards, check with manufacturer for latest information.

Michael Ponce de Leon's hydraulic press, made by Charles Brand, can exert tremendous pressure in a vertical motion, enabling the artist to print very deeply embossed bas-relief plates.

Charles Brand 30" by 50" motorized etching press with micrometers and blotter storage shelf. Studio Romano-Ross.

Brand 24" by 46" geared etching press, no micrometers, springs holding roller off bed. Chain is normally covered with steel box.

Laszlo (Rembrandt) 24″ by 42″ geared etching press. Covered chain drive, #1376.

Rembrandt etching press, 28″ by 48″, with 36″ dia-circular drive wheel. G-1 gearing, #1411.

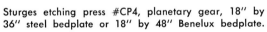

Sturges etching press #CP4, planetary gear, 18″ by 36″ steel bedplate or 18″ by 48″ Benelux bedplate.

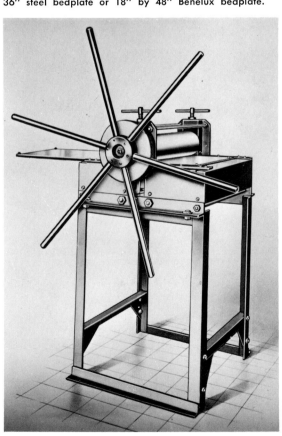

Sturges etching press #CP5, 28″ by 48″, steel bed, 8-1 planetary gear. Calibrated adjustment gauges are available.

Dickerson Combination press, 27" by 48", prints etchings and lithos with changeable top roller and scraper bar. Motorized only. Lightweight. Available from Graphic Chemical.

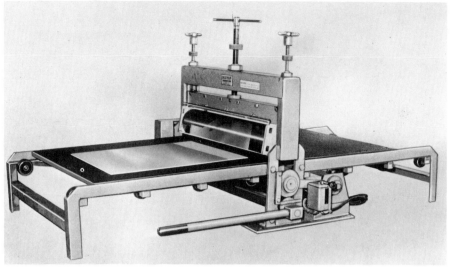

Glen Alps, motorized model "B" etching press, 40" by 66" steel bed, large rollers. Also available in a geared model hand driven by a large wheel.

Meeker McFee, motorized etching presses, 24" by 48" printing surface, Benelux bed, shielded top roller, lightweight. University of Wisconsin.

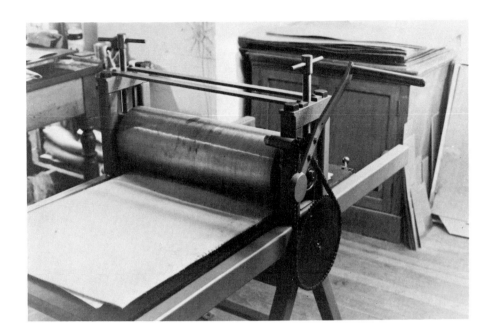

Griffen geared etching press (experimental model), 24" by 40" bed of fir plywood.

Craftool geared etching press, 24" by 40", steel bed, covered operating parts.

Old clothes wringer with wooden rollers. This press will print an etching if the depth of the line does not exceed 2/100 inch.

German press installed in Bank Street Atelier. Motorized.

American French Tool Co. 36" by 60" geared etching press has cable restraints to keep bed on press.

Craftsmen Machinery Co. (formerly Fox Graphics) make this 24" x 48" Benelux bed, geared etching press.

Fox Graphics press has 24" by 48" bed with a choice of gear ratios, 4 to 1 or 10 to 1. Benelux bed.

ETCHING PRESSES, Imported Currently Available

Manufacturer	Bed Size	Gears	Weight	Micrometers Available	Price*	Motor Available	Comments
Wilfred Kimber	8 x 14	No		No	Write	No	Available in nine models
24 Kings Bench	12 x 20	No		No	to	No	and many sizes. Solid,
Blackfriars,	16 x 24	Yes		No	manu-	No	strong presses of con-
London, S.E.1	16 x 30	Yes		No	facturer	No	ventional design. Large
England	19 x 36	Yes		No	for	No	sizes are expensive and
	19 x 36	Yes		No	latest	No	heavy.
	23 x 36	Yes		No	prices.	No	
	23 x 42	Yes		No		No	
	26 x 48	Yes		No		No	
	31 x 54	Yes		No		Yes	
	36 x 60	Yes		No		Yes	
	42 x 60	Yes		No		Yes	
Bottega D'Arte	15 x 28	No		No	690	No	
Grafica	16 x 28	Yes		No	800	No	
6 Via Degli Artisti	18 x 35	Yes		No	1100	No	
Florence, Italy	26 x 48	Yes		No	1425	No	
Sakura Color	11 x 20	No	50	No	—	No	These presses are avail-
Products Corp.	16 x 36	No	331	No	257	No	able with gears for a
1-1 Nakamichi	18 x 36	No	440	No	341	No	little more money.
Motoamachi	21 x 43	No	705	No	483	No	
Higashinari-Ku	27 x 51	No	926	No	1181	No	
Osaka, Japan	21 x 43	Yes	771	No	1291	Yes	
	27 x 51	Yes	992	No	1593	Yes	Floor models.
	40 x 85	Yes	4846	No	3968	Yes	

An 18" x 36 steel bed with a geared drive features this imported Sakura press.

SELECTED BIBLIOGRAPHY

Only the books and articles that might be useful to a working artist-printmaker are included. The literature on prints and printmaking is vast, and works that are essentially scholarly in nature are listed separately. The tabulation of monographs on individual artists is listed alphabetically by artist and is intended as source material to reveal what some of the most inspired artists throughout the centuries have done with the creative print. In general, emphasis is placed on works that are currently available as reprints.

General

Eichenberg, Fritz (editor), *Artists Proof* (Magazine and Annuals), All issues, Pratt Graphic Art Center, New York. The most complete and best-produced survey of contemporary printmaking.

Getlein, Frank and Dorothy, *The Bite of the Print*, Clarkson N. Potter, Inc., New York 1963. A sympathetic and enthusiastic outline of satire and irony in prints.

Gilmour, Pat, *Modern Prints*, Studio Vista|Dutton Pictureback, London, 1970. A small format survey of contemporary prints.

Hayter, Stanley William, *About Prints*, Oxford University Press, London 1962. A innovator in contemporary printmaking discusses some aspects of the field.

Ivins, William, *How Prints Look*, Beacon Hill, paperback 1943. Analysis and enlargements of techniques by an expert.

Ivins, William, *Prints and Visual Communication*, DaCapo reprint, New York 1969. Some fascinating insights into prints as information bearers.

Karshan, Donald, *American Printmaking*, Smithsonian Institution Press 1969. A readable, historical survey.

Karshan, Donald, *Language of the Print*, Chanticleer Press, New York, Random House, 1968. Selections from a remarkable, recently acquired collection of master prints.

Mayor, A. Hyatt, *Prints and People*, Metropolitan Museum of Art, New York 1971. A brilliant and witty survey of prints, written with great style by the Curator Emeritus of the Metropolitan.

Roger-Marx, Claude, *Graphic Art of the Nineteenth Century*, McGraw-Hill, New York 1962. Informative, brilliant discussion of an intensely interesting period in printmaking. Small format.

Sachs, Paul J., *Modern Prints and Drawings*, Knopf, New York 1954. Small format, readable, well-chosen illustrations.

Sotriffer, Kristan, *Printmaking, History and Technique*, McGraw-Hill, New York 1968. A good, general introduction to the history of printmaking. Some worthwhile illustrations.

Zigrosser, Carl, *The Book of Fine Prints*, Crown Publishers, New York 1956. A classic short history of printmaking. Clear, readable text, small reproductions.

Zigrosser, Carl, *Multum in Parvo*, G. Braziller, New York 1965. An appreciation of miniature prints.

General Techniques

Brunner, Felix, *A Handbook of Graphic Reproduction Processes*, Visual Communication Books, Hastings House, New York. Highly useful. Good layout and design.

Heller, Jules, *Printmaking Today*, University of Southern California 1965, Revised 1971. Elementary survey of print techniques.

Peterdi, Gabor, *Printmaking*, Macmillan 1971. Recently updated, this is one of the most useful books on the intaglio processes by a creative and innovative artist.

Intaglio Techniques

Bosse, A., *Traicte' des Manieres de Graver en taille-douce*, Revised by Cochin in Paris 1745, 1758. Illustrated technique of engraving and etching.

Brunsdon, John, *The Technique of Etching and Engraving*, Reinhold, New York 1965. Straightforward, direct exposition of processes and methods.

Buckland-Wright, John, *Etching and Engraving*, Studio Publications, London 1953. First-rate work book; still very valuable.

Gross, Anthony, *Etching, Engraving and Intaglio Printing*, Oxford, New York and London 1970. Mainly traditional methods.

Hayter, Stanley William, *New Ways of Gravure*, Oxford, New York and London 1966. The intaglio methods, explained by Hayter.

Lalanne, Maxime, *A Treatise on Etching*, Estes and Lauriat, Boston 1885. Still has much useful material for the artist.

Lumsden, E. S., *The Art of Etching*, Dover reprint, paperback, New York. First published 1922. Witty, knowledgeable, and helpful to the serious student.

Morrow, B. F., *The Art of Aquatint*, G. P. Putnam's Sons, New York 1935. Practical approach to traditional methods.

Pennell, Joseph, *Etchers and Etching*, Macmillan, New York 1931. Reflections by an admirer of Whistler.

Monographs on Artists
(Listed alphabetically by artist)

Leonard Baskin, The Graphic Work 1950–60, FAR Gallery, New York 1970.

Bonnard Lithographe, by Claude Roger-Marx, Andre Sauret, Monte Carlo 1952.

Georges Braque; His Graphic Work, by W. Hofmann, Harry Abrams, New York.

Bresdin, Rodolphe, by K. G. Boon, Amsterdam 1955. A fantacist of the highest rank whose lithographs are well worth study.

Graphic Works of Peter Brueghel the Elder, by A. Klein, Paperback Dover 1963.

Jacques Callot, by Edwin De. T. Bechtel, Braziller, New York 1955.

The Graphic Art of Mary Cassat, by Donald Karshan, Smithsonian Institution 1967.

Marc Chagall, His Graphic Work, by Franz Meyer, Harry Abrams, New York.

The Fantastic Engravings of Wendel Dietterlin, Dover reprint, paperback. Inventive, baroque architectural studies.

Durer, Complete Engravings, Etchings, and Woodcuts, by Karl-Adolf Knappe, Harry Abrams, New York.

The Graphic Art of M. C. Escher, Meredith Press 1961. A craftsman of the first rank creates some ingenious illusions with incredible precision.

Der Liebesspiegel (Gavarni), by E. Wieser, Aehren Verlag Affaltern 1953.

Goya Caprichos, by M. Micko, Spring Books, London.

Complete Etchings of Goya, Crown, New York 1943.

Wood Engravings of Winslow Homer, by B. Gelman, Crown, New York 1969.

Kirchner, His Graphic Art, by Annemarie Dube-Heynig, New York Graphic Society 1961. Many well-printed, large color plates.

Prints and Drawings of Kathe Kollwitz, by Carl Zigrosser, Dover, paperback, 1969.

Marino Marini, Graphic Work and Paintings, Harry Abrams, New York.

Joan Miro, His Graphic Work, by Sam Hunter, Harry Abrams, New York.

Rolf Nesch, Universe Books, New York 1969. A presentation of the work of a fresh creative spirit.

The Graphic Art of Rolf Nesch, Detroit Institute Arts 1969 paperback. Excellent catalog covers a retrospective of the innovator of collage prints.

Pablo Picasso: Fifty-five years of his graphic work, Harry Abrams, New York 1965.

Picasso: Sixty Years of Graphic Works, Introductions by D-H Kahnweiler and B. Geiser, Los Angeles County Mus. of Art paper. Catalog of a large exhibition, well illustrated.

Jose Guadalupe Posada, Hans Secker, Verlag der Kunst Dresden 1961.

Odilon Redon, by Andre Mellerio, Da Capo Press New York 1968. Reprint of a standard work.

The Graphic Works of Odilon Redon, Dover, paperback New York 1969.

Rembrandt, by K. G. Boon, Harry Abrams. Good reproductions.

The Complete Engravings of Martin Schongauer, by Alan Shestack, Dover paperback 1969.

E. Vuillard, L'Oeuvre Gravé, by Claude Roger Marx, Andre Sauret, Monte Carlo 1952.

Ward, Lynd, God's Man, A Novel in Woodcuts, Johnathan Cape and Harrison Smith, New York 1929.

Scholarly Treatises

Delteil, Loys, *Le Peintre-Graveur Illustre'*, Collector's Editions, New York Reprint of 32 columes, Major work of 19th-century and early 20th-century French artists.

Dortu, M. G., *Toulouse-Lautrec et son oeuvre*, Collector's Editions, New York 1970 6 volume reprint.

Harris, Jean, *Edouard Manet, Graphic Works: A Definite Catalogue Raisonne*, Collector's Editions, New York 1970 reprint.

Hind, Arthur M., *A Catalog of Rembrandt's Etchings*, Da Capo reprint in two volumes. 1967.

Hind, Arthur M., *A History of Engraving and Etching from the 15th century* to 1914, Dover reprint, paperback. Many astute observations and evaluations.

Hind, Arthur M., *An Introduction to the History of Woodcut*, Dover reprint, in two volumes, paperback.

Hollstein, F. W. H., *Dutch & Flemish Etchings, Engravings & Woodcuts, 1450–1700*, Menno Hertzberger, Amsterdam, various dates in 19 volumes. A detailed survey of an enormous body of work.

Hollstein, F. W. H., *German Engravings, Etchings & Woodcuts 1400–1700*, Menno Hertzberger, Amsterdam, various dates in 7 volumes. A thorough and effective study of the scene. A monumental work.

Laran, *Jean, L'Estampe*, Presses Universitaires de France, 1959 in 2 volumes. Beautifully printed, with large heliogravure and color reproductions.

Lehrs, Max, *History and Critical Catalog of German, Netherlandish and French Copper Engravings in the 15th Century*, Collector's Edition, New York 1970. Reprint of 9 volumes.

Lehrs, Max, *Late Gothic Engravings of Germany and the Netherlands*, Dover paperback 1969. Marvelous source material for this era.

Lieure, Jules, *Jacques Callot: La Vie Artisique et Catalogue Raissone*, Collectors Editions, New York 1970. Reprint of 9 volumes.

Massar, Phyllis Dearborn, *Stefano della Bella: Catalogue Raisonne*, Collectors Edition reprint, New York 1970—two volumes.

Minott, Charles I., *The Engravings of Martin Schongauer: Studies and Illustrated Catalogue*, Collectors Edition Reprint, New York 1970.

Mourlot, Fernand, *Picasso Lithographe 1919–1956*, Monte Carlo: Andre Sauret 1949–1964 4 vols. Beautifully printed but rare and expensive because original lithos are included.

Panofsky, Erwin, *Albecht Durer*, Princeton, 1943 2 vols. The definitive study of Durer and his work.

INDEX